THE SPIRIT
OF MASONRY

THE SPIRIT OF MASONRY

by

WILLIAM HUTCHINSON

Introduction by Trevor Stewart

THE AQUARIAN PRESS

First published 1775
This edition first published 1987

© THE AQUARIAN PRESS 1987

British Library Cataloguing in Publication Data

Hutchinson, William
The spirit of masonry.—(Masonic classics
· series)
1. Freemasonry
I. Title   II. Series
366.1   HS395

ISBN 0-85030-531-4

*The Aquarian Press is part of the
Thorsons Publishing Group,
Wellingborough, Northamptonshire,
NN8 2RQ, England*

Printed in Great Britain by Woolnough Bookbinding,
Irthlingborough, Northamptonshire

3 5 7 9 10 8 6 4 2

MASONIC CLASSICS SERIES

FREEMASONRY has an extensive literature but much of it, having been written for a specialized readership and published in short runs, is now out of print. This series has been designed to provide both the serious student and the general reader with an opportunity of reading a wide cross section of classic works on Freemasonry. It is proposed to include standard historical works which have influenced the historiography of Freemasonry by authors such as Sadler, Hughan, Oliver, and Gould; texts basic to an understanding of Freemasonry, such as the Old Charges and Constitutions; contemporary handbooks and commentaries produced to explain Freemasonry to its members such as the works of Preston, Hutchinson and Calcott; and Masonic oddities such as MacKenzie's idiosyncratic *Royal Masonic Cyclopaedia*.

Each volume will consist of a facsimile of the original text, or the best edition if more than one was published, prefaced by a critical introduction by an acknowledged authority on the subject. The introduction will describe the author of the text and place him and his work in the context of its time and its relevance to the development of Freemasonry or its historiography.

JOHN HAMILL
Series Editor

INTRODUCTION

WILLIAM HUTCHINSON was born in Durham City, at 10 Owengate, on 31 December 1732, second child and eldest son of William Hutchinson (1705–1777), a well-respected attorney and later JP. The paternal side of his family all originated from Cornforth near Bishop Middleham while his mother, Hannah (1707–1790) was from Butterby three miles out of the city. The family was respectable enough to be entitled to entries in early editions of Burke's *Landed Gentry*. Judging from early letters in the 'Honourable Love' MSS collection, Hutchinson appears to have enjoyed a close, affectionate relationship with both parents and the atmosphere of cheerful companionship and obvious delight in the company of each sibling radiates throughout the letters.

It is very likely that Hutchinson and his younger brother, Robert (1750–1773), were educated at the Durham Cathedral Grammar school because of its proximity to the family home although no evidence that either attended there has survived. The master-in-charge when Hutchinson would have probably attended was Richard Dongworth (1703–1761), a graduate of Magdalene College, Cambridge. Dongworth was a man of some academic standing for he was offered the head-mastership of his *alma mater*, Eton College, while he was at Durham. He showed that he was also a man of some character by resisting the temptation to move south, declining the better position, and remaining at Durham

until his death. A contemporary, Thomas Gyll, noted
in his diary in 1761 that Dongworth was 'a learned and
polite gentleman with a reputation for temperance,
noteworthy in an age of regular imbibing'. The usher was
Thomas Randall, another Etonian and a graduate of
Corpus Christi College, Oxford. He was appointed
master after Dongworth, and held the position until 1768.
Randall was an indefatigible antiquary and collector of
MSS, especially those relating to the history of the
Durham diocese. He retired to Eglingham in
Northumberland, continued his researches into the
northern parishes and bequeathed twenty huge volumes
of MSS to George Allan, FSA (1736–1800) who donated
them to Hutchinson. These were used extensively for
the *State of the Churches in Northumberland* and in the
History of Durham.

His teachers clearly exercised a powerful and lasting
influence on the youthful Hutchinson. The love of
classical and historical learning acquired early in life never
left him. Latin and Greek quotations, historical allusions
and classical references proliferate throughout his writings,
sometimes not very accurately. Quotations from no less
than thirteen different Greek and Latin writers are
scattered liberally in footnotes in *The Spirit of Masonry*.
Druidical worship, Egyptian mysteries, Pythagoras,
Solomon's temple, the Jewish Tabernacle and Celtic
religion are topics supported by quotations from previous
authors in the published text but not in the original
manuscript. While educated gentlemen were expected
to show some interest and accomplishment in such
subjects, during the latter half of the eighteenth century
there was a widespread supposition that superficial

learning could lead to pedantry. Hutchinson was often accused by contemporary reviewers of his antiquarian publications that he was pedantic. Moreover, his historical conjectures were sometimes alleged to be both quite unoriginal and inaccurate. Be that as it probably is, a grammar school education, such as Hutchinson probably received, was recognized as having many advantages, not the least of which was the supposition that it was a powerful promoter of virtue and of spiritual ennobling. More particularly, history enabled the diligent scholar to profit morally from the previous experience of others and Hutchinson certainly showed a marked tendency to draw moral lessons from historical incidents and his surroundings. He was not unusual in this practice although it did not endear him to some contemporary London critics who were early promoters of a more objective approach to historical writing. At any rate, he was in no doubt of the lasting value of the education he received. He wrote (in *Poems on Severall Occasions*):

> From thence we gain
> The doctrine which through life shall ever reign;
> Too deep to change, so rooted in the mind
> Reside it, ev'ry maxim is confined.
> A prejudice that Time cannot subdue.

Hutchinson followed his father into the legal profession. Attorneys then were constant figures of fun, witness the many, often vicious, satirical cartoons in the magazines, popular farces like Richard Cumberland's *The Country Attorney* (1787), libellous allegations in *The Gentleman's Magazine* and William Richardson's anonymous poem *The Newcastle Attornies, or Villainy Displayed* (1809) issued

'Pro Bono Publico'. Nevertheless, in an era of increasing urbanization, more widely shared material prosperity, sophistication and heightened consciousness of social status, the professions, as we know them, began to emerge and they offered a unique vehicle of upward social mobility not least because of their sheer carrying capacity. Among the foremost of these professions were the attorneys whose numbers swelled in response to the ever increasing demand for a greater range and variety of services. Hutchinson was almost certainly trained initially in his father's own office, so saving the not inconsiderable cost of indentures. Thereafter, he was sent, quite unusually for the Northern provinces, to complete his training in London as an apprentice to a practising attorney there. Unfortunately, the PRO Stamp Register for the relevant years is now missing so we cannot tell who was responsible for the 'finishing off'. Nor are we able to have any confidence in the quality of the training which he underwent, for often the training generally was routine and haphazard and judges' oral examinations of intending practitioners were perfunctory. However, according to the 'Honourable Love' MS, Hutchinson himself was left in no doubt of the debt which he owed to his father in paying for this valuable London experience.

On his return to the North East in about 1755–6, Hutchinson was set up by his father in a newly vacated legal practice in the prosperous market town of Barnard Castle. He arrived one dismal, wet February day and he viewed the prospect of his exile there with considerable alarm at first, especially after experiencing the bright life of London. But he settled quickly into the much smaller community. On marrying Elizabeth Marshall of Stockton on 30 September 1758, he purchased a large house, The Grove, in Gallowgate and the couple continued to live there for the rest of their lives raising their ever increasing family. His practice began to grow. Recent studies of demographic trends in County Durham from the middle of the sixteenth century to the end of the eighteenth show beyond doubt that Durham, Darlington, Staindrop and Barnard Castle, plus the ports of Stockton and Hartlepool, all experienced their greatest rates of population increase in the 1700s. The 1801 Census shows Barnard Castle as the township with the largest population in the Darlington Ward of the County. These trends were mirrored in the rising number of turnpike trusts, enclosures of waste or moor lands, and coal, lead and copper mining operations undertaken during that century in that part of the county. Advertisements concerning all of these proliferated in all of the local newspapers. Consequently, there were ample opportunities for an ambitious young attorney to develop a flourishing legal practice there where competition from other attorneys was negligible in the late 1750s.

Hutchinson's first reactions to the small market town on the moors were chronicled in one of the early letters in his *Honourable Love* MS. He wrote: 'It is very populous and very dirty . . . the buildings in general are old and very melancholy . . . The wind blew bitter northwest, sharp hail rattled on our hats and a gloomy sky seemed to drag its ragged skirts along the drenched hills. The people looked boorish and the clang of the death bell grated on the ear the tale of mortality, for there is a disease in the town which hurrys [sic] off hundreds, proceeding xii The SPIRIT of MASONRY

from a scarcity of bread . . . I did not like the people
I confess . . .'. But he was made to feel welcome and
he changed his opinions, of both the place and the people,
quickly.

As his legal practice grew in size and complexity his
love of his new surroundings deepened. The wild moors,
the tree-lined lanes and the River Tees with the waterfall
at High Force figure prominently in several of his prose
and verse works (eg. *The Hermitage*; *A Week in a Cottage*;
The Tears of Bellville Vale etc.). Soon after his marriage,
in addition to his private legal practice, he was appointed
Clerk to the County Lieutenancy when the County
Volunteer Militia was reorganized and, as such, he was
involved in the minutiae of administering that force.
Consequently, he became something of a power in the
County Palatine. The Durham Volunteer Militia began
service in February, 1760 and Hutchinson's many quasi-
military duties included arranging the quarterly
musterings, making recruitment tours, compiling muster
lists and adjudicating on claims for exemption from
service. At a time of constant fears of foreign invasion,
recurrent Jacobite rebellion, increasing unrest amongst
the artisan and agricultural labouring classes, Hutchinson's
social eminence improved for he no doubt played some
part in occasionally suppressing such civil unrest using
the volunteer militia.

This work drew him to the attention of the then second
Earl of Darlington, Henry Vane, Lord Barnard, so it was
understandable that he should thereafter be appointed
Steward of the Earl's Manor of Barnard Castle for a time.
The many duties of land stewards in the eighteenth
century have been well documented. Suffice it to point

out that Hutchinson was an obvious choice as an up and coming attorney with a London training. He would have come into daily contact with a wide cross-section of local society, from the Earl to tenants. His remuneration was fairly substantial for, in addition to the usual 5 per cent commission from all collected rents, there were arbitration fees, attendance fees at local manorial courts, brokerage fees in respect of larger transactions of leases, turnpike trusts and the enclosures of the Barnard Castle moors. This busy life was pursued unremittingly with accuracy and discretion until he was quite old. There are many traces of his involvement in various kinds of legal activities. As a country attorney he became an important figure in local society for his professional concerns placed him constantly at the centre of affairs. By the end of the century it was not unknown for attorneys, like Hutchinson, to be found among the more energetic leaders of a greatly enriched provincial life. It is not surprising, therefore, to find him in 1809–10, taking a leading role in a remarkable controversy against the then Bishop of Durham, Dr Shute Barrington (1734–1826) which centred on whether the Bishop, as Custos Rotulorum of the County Palatine, had the right to decline to consent to the reappointment of JPs if he considered, as chief local magistrate, they were unworthy of holding further office.

Sometime prior to 1771 Hutchinson was fortunate in gaining the friendship of George Allan. This wealthy attorney and amateur publisher of Blackwell Grange, Darlington was an important influence on Hutchinson's life. He inherited Randall's MSS and augmented the collection considerably by purchasing others, including the natural history collection of another neighbouring antiquary and naturalist, Marmaduke Tunstall FSA (1743–1790). Allan and Tunstall sponsored Hutchinson's candidature for membership of the newly formed London Society of Antiquaries in 1781. More particularly, Allan prompted Hutchinson to undertake the compilation of a history of the County Palatine, a project which Allan had long cherished. He wrote to a Dr Henry of Edinburgh University: 'Neither having leisure nor health to finish the work, [I] have consigned every paper to my industrious friend, Mr Hutchinson, who will usher it into the world . . .'.

So Hutchinson embarked on the historical enterprises that were to dominate the rest of his life. (A full list of Hutchinson's writings appears as Appendix I.) They were obviously a source of much private pleasure — witness the loving care he continued to exercise in annotating and illustrating his personal copy of the *History of Durham* long after its publication. (The copy is now in the Chapter Library of Durham Cathedral.) Yet they were also sources of much public bitterness and controversy. There were repeated and somewhat vitriolic published criticisms from various historians of Hutchinson's writings. A lengthy correspondence in the *Gentleman's Magazine*, for instance, is just one indication of how poorly his labours were received. It is true that they brought him into useful contact with notable illustrators like John Bailey, Joseph Collyer jun., Issac Gassett, sen., and, of course, Thomas Bewick. They also enabled him to become acquainted with more superior intellects like Francis Grose and Thomas Pennant. However, it is also true that the preoccupation with writing about local history led to his later impoverishment. There was an unfortunate and costly legal wrangle with Solomon Hodgson, the Newcastle publisher of the first two volumes of the *History of Durham*, about the subscription monies and the late delivery of the enormously augmented MS. The case was arbitrated against Hutchinson. The completed sets of three volumes did not sell nearly so well as Hutchinson and his new printer, Francis Jollie of Carlisle, had anticipated. The London publisher and bookseller, John Nichols, bought up most of the remaining sets but these were destroyed in a disastrous fire at his Red Lion Passage warehouse and Hutchinson never recovered financially. Surviving correspondence shows that he had to borrow repeatedly from his friend and mentor George Allan.

Whatever disappointments and frustrations there may have been for him in his various historical enterprises, these did not deter Hutchinson from undertaking other literary tasks. Indeed, as one contemporary, Thomas Bell, wrote: 'he had an inveterate itch for the drama'. His first effort was an early draft of *Baleazar, King of Tyre*, a five-act tragedy of 1758. He returned to the subject of justifying rebellion against a cruel tyrant thirty years later and produced a quite different longer version, variously entitled *Pygmalion, King of Tyre* and *Baleazar, King of Tyre* in 1788.

By this time Hutchinson had become acquainted with the Revd. Dr Daniel Watson (1718–1804), Rector of Middleton Tyas from 1767 until his death, who produced detailed written comments on the text. The rector did not seem to have been very impressed with Hutchinson's efforts for he urged the would-be dramatist to direct his talent to producing plays of greater moral significance. He suggested that an anti-slavery theme would be more popular since the anti-slavery campaign was reaching one of its peaks in 1789, interest in it having been generated by the Quaker communities in Darlington and Stockton and the Methodist congregations in Newcastle. The result was *The Princess of Zanfara*, submitted for critical approval to one Revd. Dr John Carr, Master of Hertford Grammar School with whom Watson's son was being educated and whose approbation they supposed might hold some sway with Thomas Harris, proprietor/manager of the then recently refurbished Covent Garden Theatre in London. However, Harris apparently thought little of the play for he returned it quickly with the criticism that it was too much like Thomas Southern's very popular *Oroonko*. In spite of this abrupt critical rebuff by an acknowledged arbiter of popular theatrical taste, Hutchinson was not deterred. He published *The Princess of Zanfara* anonymously at first. Hutchinson's obituary claims that it was thereafter performed in northern theatres to some success but there is no mention in the records of the Lord Chamberlain's Office of it having been submitted there for approval nor in the surviving records of important provincial theatres like the Theatre Royal, Newcastle and the Georgian Theatre, Richmond, Yorkshire, is there evidence of the play having been performed in either place. Yet it must have been performed somewhere for in the Bowes Museum collection a prompt copy has survived with stage manager's MS annotations and deletions. The quality of the play is somewhat questionable. It does lack originality in theme and is somewhat sentimental in its treatment of the controversial subject. Nevertheless, Hutchinson persisted and issued a superior, second edition in 1792 under his own name but this fared even worse, the greatest part of the impression being used eventually as waste paper.

Hutchinson tried novels and verse too. His poetry survives in scattered MSS and some small published collections. It is largely of a lyrical, Romantic and moralistic vein, its themes being those that are typical of the eighteenth century: Reason, love, death, nature, the 'Summum Bonum', society and the benefits of a pastoral existence. The published fiction (*The Hermitage*, *The Doubtful Marriage* and *A Week at a Cottage*) was written explicitly for similar didactic purposes. The impulse to instruct was clearly one which Hutchinson found impossible to resist. There are many passages in which he enunciates moral lessons from landscape and ancient ruins even in his purely antiquarian books.

It was understandable, that, as a rising young attorney with an expanding circle of social connections, Hutchinson should become a Freemason, and records have survived that show him taking an active part in the deliberations of the local Vestry meetings from 1769 onwards. He was initiated on 4 June 1770 as a member of an unnamed 'Moderns' lodge which then met at the Hare and Hounds and sometimes at the Square and Compasses in Barnard Castle. This Lodge of Concord, as it became known in 1785, was actually constituted in 1773 though the Warrant of Confirmation (1819) stated that the Lodge had held a Warrant dated November, 1770 No. 406. There had been a previous lodge, Sun Lodge No. 243, constituted on 21 April 1759, which also met at the Square and Compasses but it was erased on 27 January 1768. Apart from being the market town for the area, Barnard Castle also had a thriving carpet weaving industry so it was understandable that a lodge should emerge there and that a small group of like-minded citizens should persist in forming a lodge in spite of the brief interregnum 1768–70, it being a not unreasonable assumption that some members of the earlier lodge established a replacement in 1770. The new lodge had close connections with brethren of neighbouring lodges (eg. No. 242 in Richmond — later named 'Lennox' and No. 210 in Darlington — later named 'Restoration'). These lodges held joint masonic processions in full regalia in Barnard Castle as early as 1771 and Hutchinson took an active part in these.

Hutchinson became probably the most notable master of this Lodge of Concord. He claimed to have held the office on several occasions and this is confirmed by the few surviving records which show that he was presiding over the lodge's affairs in 1771, 1773, and 1776. He was also a founder and the first master of the Raby Lodge No. 461 (warranted 6 November 1784 but erased 4 April 1798). He had something of a high opinion of his own masonic worthiness, however. After the publication of the first edition of *The Spirit of Masonry* he confided to James Hesletine, then Grand Secretary, in a letter dated 30 December 1775, that he would like to be appointed to the vacant Provincial Grand mastership of Durham and he was confident that those lodges with which he was acquainted would support his self-nomination. He actually petitioned Lord Petre, the then Grand Master, for the appointment on the same day. In the event, he was unsuccessful. In 1785, however, William White, Hesletine's successor as Grand Secretary suggested that he offer himself again for the newly vacant post but he declined probably because he was embroiled then in the protracted and costly legal wrangle with Solomon Hodgson.

Hutchinson was active masonically from the earliest days of his masonic career. He took a leading part in the 1771 procession referred to above. On 5 July 1773, while on a tour of the Lake District with his brother, Robert, collecting materials for his *Excursion to the Lakes*, he attended a meeting of the Kendal Lodge No. 256 (later named Union Lodge) and was invited to deliver an oration on masonry by the brethren there. The Kendal masons minuted in their records that they paid him 6d for 'an oration of Masonry from B'd Castle'. Perhaps this was Hutchinson's Rokeby oration (see below) already in print. By 19 July he had returned home to take the lead in the formal procession in full regalia from the lodge room in the market square to the banks of the River Tees to lay the foundation stone of the new Abbey Bridge on the Rokeby estate. The project was financed by the new owner of the Rokeby manor house, John Sawrey Morritt. After the stone was laid, the brethren entered a large tent where, to a mixed audience of masons and non-masons, Hutchinson delivered 'an excellent lecture which gave great satisfaction'. The oration was considered worthy of publication by a masonic printer, one John Sadler of Darlington, and it sold rapidly at 6d a copy, the proceeds being donated by Hutchinson to charity.

Hutchinson visited several other lodges in County Durham. For instance, on 7 March 1775 he visited the lodge in the city, then No. 245, which became known as Marquis of Granby Lodge in 1782. He presented the brethren with a copy of his recently published *The Spirit of Masonry* on that occasion and early inventories show that it remained a valued part of the lodge's collections until at least 1782. Such was his reputation as a speaker that he was invited by the brethren of a Sunderland lodge, then No. 136, to deliver, on 16 July 1778, an oration in the presence of the then Provincial Grand Master, Captain George Thompson. The occasion was the dedication of the new lodge rooms in Vine Street. A contemporary reviewer commented that the speech was 'a learned and ingenious display of the antiquity and importance of Free Masonry'. It was published simultaneously as a pamphlet in London, Newcastle and Sunderland and was thought to be of such merit that it was translated quickly into Dutch and published in Leyden in 1780. There is other, perhaps more questionable, testimony of Hutchinson's prowess as a masonic orator. Oliver's *Revelations of a Square* (1855) is an account of a nationwide tour made by Hesletine in about 1769. It comments that Barnard Castle masonry was 'shining with unsullied lustre under the active superintendence of Brother Hutchinson, who . . . delivered his own lectures, and orations . . . and his example was followed by the Masters of other lodges who visited the Barnard Castle lodge for the advantage of his instructions . . . [which] were so much admired for the pure principles of Masonry which they en-unciated . . .'.

The Spirit of Masonry originated in Hutchinson's lectures to his own Barnard Castle brethren. In submitting a first

draft of his MS for the approval of the Premier Grand
Lodge, he wrote to Hesletine on 9 February 1774: 'At
the instance of several of my Brethren I have been
induced to transcribe a small book of Moral Lectures
on Masonry.' He observed that: 'the lectures were
composed for our lodge only [but] when some visiting
brethren were with us, their publication was desired
. . .'. The intention was for Hesletine to submit the text
to Grand Lodge for approval which would enhance the
sales. Hutchinson went on: 'I flatter myself you will find
the contents of the book not only curious and many of
the matters therein new, but also that it is calculated for
the honour of Masonry . . .'.

We may suppose that the MS was duly read, possibly
by William Preston himself, (1742–1818), who was by
then Deputy Grand Secretary, assisting Hesletine in his
attorney's chambers at Doctors' Commons. It did not,
however, meet with automatic approval for Hutchinson
had to write four months later (27 June 1774) to Hesletine
when he submitted an amended MS: 'I have altered it
throughout and introduced every sentence sent me in
the written comments. I flatter myself, on revisal, no
objection will be made to my publishing. The note I
received [and] introduced some new [ones] which I think
greatly improve the work.'

A copy of the original draft MS was donated by a Miss
L. McLean to Grand Lodge Library in 1908. It bears
an initialled MS note in Hutchinson's own handwriting:
'This book was presented to the Grand Lodge for a
sanction in the year 1774 but was not permitted to be
published without such alterations as was [sic] prescribed.'
By comparing it with the first published edition it is

possible to infer the content of these written comments, notes or alterations to which Hutchinson referred and we can judge the nature and extent of the proposed changes which Grand Lodge authorities required before the desired Sanction was granted. It would seem that Hutchinson's original text was a more modest affair then the sanctioned first edition. Yet it is worthwhile recalling that the 'imprimatur' would hardly have been forthcoming if his theories had been much at variance with Grand Lodge thinking at that time. Moreover, all of the major variations are additions, not deletions, which also indicates that what Hutchinson produced originally, although not entirely complete with regard to the historical origins of Freemasonry as perceived by them, did not raise any substantial objection from within Grand Lodge.

Hutchinson having made the necessary changes, the reason why the Premier Grand Lodge granted the very unusual sanction was that the book served their purposes. It may have been intended to play a part in lending Freemasonry some much needed respectability at a time when many scurrilous attacks on the Craft had entertained the non-masonic public at large. Freemasonry was widely and almost constantly ridiculed in the popular press. The general tenor of the required additions was an attempt to demonstrate ancient origins and therefore social acceptability by reference to classical and biblical literature and to ancient history. The claim to social respectability derived from alleged antiquity was intended to be further reinforced by the reprinting of the Locke-Leland MS as an Appendix. This was clearly not part of Hutchinson's own scheme for he did not use the MS in his original draft and its inclusion was almost certainly made at Premier Grand Lodge's behest. Of course, the Locke-Leland MS is now widely recognized in masonic circles as being spurious but throughout the eighteenth century it remained popular and intriguing and it appeared in several notable publications. Perhaps the aim in sanctioning publication was also to counter more informed and more effective criticisms, such as those of the Northern Associate Synod. No doubt the continuing conflict with the Antients' Grand Lodge was a factor in persuading Petre *et alii* to try to counter their opponents' more organized system of lodges by assisting recruitment to membership of lodges nationwide. Moreover, the Moderns were then completing a new Freemasons' Hall in Great Queen Street after incurring huge debts to finance the ambitious building programme. Anything, such as this intended book, that might prompt brethren to subscribe much needed contributions to the sluggish Hall Fund would have been very welcome.

In 1775 the prevailing national trends within the Moderns were very unsatisfactory. There was wide-spread discontent in the provinces at the continuing haphazard lack of leadership from London in spite of the timely and necessary improvements in routine administration made by Hesletine. Grand Lodge officers rarely visited private lodges and a succession of Grand Masters had neglected their duties almost entirely. The Craft appeared to have lost a much-needed 'sense of direction' for nearly one quarter of the lodges had stopped meeting by the 1760s and had consequently been erased. A clear signal from London was needed to show the existing provincial brethren that they were not being forgotten. Fortunately, Lord Petre (*c*.1741/2–1801) was a diligent Grand Master and he, and his co-signatories of the Sanction, could have intended the book as a rallying call to the faint-hearted. From evidence available to date it seems that by *c*.1780 the numbers of provincial lodges stabilized and thereafter increased steadily. Perhaps the appearance of Hutchinson's book played some part in this trend.

Membership of the Moderns' lodges needed to be increased, especially as the rival Antients were better organized and were attracting and retaining increasing members. Hutchinson's book may have been intended to attract more and better-educated men who had more than just a passing interest in the Craft as merely just another club. Certainly the annual returns from most of the lodges in County Durham at that time, for instance, show a steady increase in the numbers of attorneys, surveyors, booksellers, newspaper printers and 'gentlemen' who became members and went on to achieve office.

Two of the Antients' charges against the Moderns were that Lectures were no longer being given at lodge meetings and that their ritual had been deliberately de-Christianized. Perusal of any of the surviving Minute Books will confirm that lectures by Masters were very rare occurrences indeed. Perhaps Grand Lodge hoped that Hutchinson's book would serve as a useful primer for those masters who were without the necessary expertise or time to produce their own lectures 'for the instruction and improvement of Craftsmen'. After 1775 circumstances seem to have improved for by 1785 John Noorthouck, then Deputy Grand Secretary, could boast in the fifth edition of the *Book of Constitutions* about 'the flourishing state of our lodges where regular instruction and suitable exercises are ever ready for all brethren who zealously aspire to improve in masonical knowledge'. Of course, he may have been boasting too!

As far as the alleged de-Christianization is concerned, the book may have been intended by Grand Lodge to refute that accusation in an academically respectable way for it purports to demonstrate once again that profound religious themes, with very long traditions, form integral parts of Freemasonry, particularly in the Third, or Master Masons', Degree.

In the first half of the eighteenth century English Freemasonry was not only organizationally weak. There was some moral potentiality but it had not yet been developed fully into intellectual strength. Its fundamental ethical principles were too feeble to unify it into a lasting structure. It is now widely acknowledged that the Craft's primary philosophic needs then were four. Its existing rudimentary moral principles, fraternal love and charity, needed strengthening by the addition of others. It required justification as a moral institution, the main aim of which was the inculcation of ethical conduct. Its philosophical principles needed systematizing. The prevailing, though fundamentally mistaken, intellectualist tendency of the age wanted to establish ethics on as sound a basis as the Newtonian physical laws. The search was for the same kind of axioms that were just as indisputable and similarly systematized, a kind of moral geometry. In pointing them out to the unenlightened, the bases of morality would be so self-evidently clear that they would require a man's unbiased reason to give its assent.

It is surely not without significance that freemasons conceived of God as 'the Grand Geometrician of the Universe'. (Of course, what authors like Hutchinson failed to realize in this search was that Newton's laws were merely descriptive and not prescriptive so they confused 'is' with 'ought'.) Finally, there was an urgent need to encourage Freemasonry's nascent speculative and symbolical tendencies for, as Sir Leslie Stephen pointed out shrewdly in his *History of English Thought in the Eighteenth Century*, the moral and religious principles to which men ostensibly adhere to do not become influential on their conduct until the doctrines have generated an imaginative symbolism.

To each of these needs Hutchinson's *Spirit of Masonry* made a contribution by extending what had already been delineated by earlier pioneers like Clare, Leslie and Brockwell. (For instance, Hutchinson added secrecy as a basic ethical principle for freemasons.) Secondly, although he never actually defined Freemasonry in this 1775 edition though he managed to describe it fully, he stated clearly in the 1802 edition that Freemasonry 'is a moral institution' and that a mason's 'first and leading principle' is 'a due observance of moral duties and obligations'. Thirdly, he made his own attempt to systematize masonic morals, postulating the hierarchical system shown opposite.

These were not attributes present on initiation; a mason would be developed towards them. Thus underpinning Hutchinson's hierarchy is the assumption of the basic malleability of the human spirit from within society, one of the main tenets of English Enlightenment philosophy.

Finally, Hutchinson made his own, perhaps

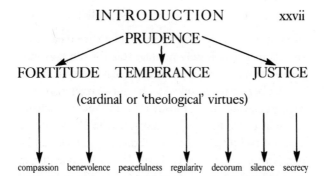

idiosyncratic, excursions into masonic symbolism. His explanations of the nature of the lodge, of its furniture and of masonic apparel and jewels are only a few examples. We may disagree with his speculations but we should be grateful that he ventured where few had gone before and where many, too numerous to mention here, have followed.

The first English edition of *The Spirit of Free Masonry* was published by John Wilkie and William Goldsmith in 1775, the same year that they issued their second, revised edition of William Preston's *Illustrations of Masonry*.

In common with contemporary practice the first edition probably ran to about 500 copies. The book was reviewed only once in the following year. The critic, possibly a Freemason himself, was not very generous. He wrote: 'Mr Hutchinson . . ., a mystic among mystics, aims not only to expound masonry as a Christian institution but to contract the privileges of the order to those Christians only who are found Trinitarians: [and] if we compare his lectures with the book of Masonical Constitutions which is published to all the world, and by which all our lodges are regulated, he will be found to display a very ostentatious parade of reading for no other purpose than to misapply it.' There is no easy way to establish how widely popular this first edition was, but it is reasonable to assume that most were purchased by members of those lodges with which Hutchinson was already acquainted: i.e., those mainly in County Durham. Certainly the Marquis of Granby Lodge in Durham itself received a copy and occasional references to it can be found in surviving records of early lodges in other distant parts of England (e.g. Union Lodge No. 320 in Bristol).

The book was popular enough to be translated into German within five years of its first appearance, being published by Stahlbaum of Berlin, who already enjoyed a reputation as a promoter of masonic and hermetic literature. Moreover, when Jollie published an augmented edition in 1795, there were nearly 600 subscribers scattered nationwide, only a minority of whom were Freemasons. This new edition was certainly popular in London to judge from a letter dated 14 February 1796 from one Simon Stephenson, London bookseller, addressed to James Field Stanfield, actor and leading member of Phoenix Lodge in Sunderland. Stephenson wrote plaintively: '. . . *The Spirit of Masonry* . . . I shall beg to know where I can procure a copy in town. By advertising it in the [Gentleman's] Magazine and other endeavours agreeable to your wishes, I could have sold a considerable number . . . the time is now gone by as my friends and other applicants have been so long disappointed.'

This expanded edition received unreserved approbation in the *Freemasons Magazine* (1797), which commented that 'Mr Hutchinson . . . has offered many ingenious conjectures upon the most intricate points of this very curious and intricate subject. If he is sometimes fanciful, he is always pleasing and instructive; and certainly a better book on the science cannot be recommended to those Brethren who wish to make themselves acquainted with the profession of which they are members.' The reviews ends by 'recommending it to all our Masonic readers, particularly to every young brother, not only on account of the charitable view which it is designed to promote, but on account of the valuable information which it contains.'

In 1800 *The Spirit of Masonry* was to spread Hutchinson's reputation as a masonic writer in the newly independent republic of America. The first American edition was identical to the 1775 issue, apart from the addition of four popular masonic songs to the Appendix. It was printed for Cottom and Stewart by Isaac Collins, an active Quaker who had moved from Burlington, Pennsylvannia, to New York in 1778 and whose printing business was by 1800 entering its final, most prosperous phase. Collins seems to have specialized in publishing books on various religious and moral topics. The edition was probably limited to the usual 500 copies. In 1800 there were only 91 private lodges holding warrants under the New York Grand Lodge. If it is assumed that each lodge purchased at least one copy and that most copies were sold, then clearly Hutchinson's readership was not restricted to just New York Freemasons. This edition of *The Spirit of Masonry* does not seem to have found its way into any of the public libraries in America, according to an anti-masonic *Catalogue of Books on the Masonic Institution in Public Libraries of 28 States of the Union* (1852).

That Hutchinson thought highly of this work himself is shown by the fact that he published no less than nine editions during his lifetime. This most unusual circumstance in pro-masonic literature of the period, exceeded only by Preston's *Illustrations*, is a clear indication of its sustained popularity. Moreover, these are different editions for Hutchinson was not content merely to reissue the original text. A careful comparison shows that he made systematic changes to the main text and augmented the footnotes. He also included in the Appendix copies of orations, songs and pamphlets, some of which were written by previous authors.

It seems that Hutchinson was never really satisfied with anything he wrote. His letters in, say, the *Gentleman's Magazine*, written in response to criticisms of his historical works, show that, although mortified, he was quite capable of defending himself against attack. There is, however, no evidence at all that he changed the texts of these books or altered his opinions in response to such criticisms. Such alterations and additions that he did make were for his own edification. For instance, after the eventual appearance of the concluding third volume of his *History of Durham*, he proceeded to make careful changes to the text and used his own new watercolour sketches to illustrate both buildings and landscape mentioned therein but not shown in the published, more professionally finished, plates. If this constant annotating was his customary practice with a work that had patently caused him so much heartache and financial impoverishment, it can be reasonably assumed that the many alterations to the text of later editions of *The Spirit of Masonry*, a much shorter work and one that he was undoubtedly proud of, were made voluntarily and with a view to enhancing the teaching.

By the time he died the work was known in England, Ireland, Scotland, Germany and America. It is a measure of its popularity and the favour with which he himself viewed it that so many different editions were published during his own lifetime (see Appendix II). This is not to say that the work gained universal praise. Critics since 1776 have been quick to point out its deficiencies: historical inaccuracies, misinterpretations of evidence, printing errors and misquotations.

One instance, from the very first page, will illustrate the kind of intriguing puzzle which Hutchinson has left us. It concerns the frontispiece which purports to be a drawing of an oval engraved beryl, allegedly an ABRAX jewel in the BM collection. The original drawing was given between pages 33 and 34 of the MS draft. It was clearly dated 1773 and initialled 'WH' by Hutchinson himself. Immediately, the attention is drawn to the discrepancy between the dates: the 1775 edition, and others, give the date when Hutchinson drew the jewel as 1769, before he was even initiated. But the mystery does not rest there. Beryls are precious stones and the one which Hutchinson claims to have seen in the BM, egg-shaped and over 1½ inches long, would qualify as, in Sotheby's terms, 'a very important jewel'. It had evidently disappeared from the BM between 1769/73 and 1790 when Tessie and Rasp were collecting material of their *Descriptive Catalogue of Ancient and Modern Engraved Gems* (1791).Beryls are hard and difficult to cut, therefore they are rarely engraved. Cabochon stones, too, are rarely engraved and, even more rarely, those doubly

cabochon (= egg shaped) like this one. Engravers prefer
to work on relatively flat surfaces. The combination of
cameo with intaglio on a convex surface is equally
surprising and the head on this cameo is unique. It
certainly escaped Worlidge's notice when he was
compiling his Catalogue in 1768. The scorpion-snake-
sun combination, at first glance, looks like good,
conventional astrology, if somewhat garbled. The
constellation of Scorpio is located surprisingly beneath
that of Ophiouchos ('the snake handler') and the sun
enters Scorpio in October so the combination could make
this gem a birthday stone, rather than an ABRAX
talisman. The 'Hebrew' engraved around the edge was
done by someone who did not know how to cut Hebrew
letters and, read as Hebrew, it makes no sense. Moreover,
beryl is traditionally the stone of Cancer, not Scorpio,
for which sardonyx, haematite and pyrites are prescribed.
The sixteenth and seventeenth centuries were great ages
for amateur astrology and home-brewed Hebrew so it
may be safer, perhaps to place Hutchinson's allegedly
ancient ABRAX jewel there rather than in second century
Gnostic Alexandria.

Modern commentators have been kinder to
Hutchinson than those of previous generations. He is
often referred to as 'the father of masonic symbolism',
'whose scholarship is just as good as Preston's, sometimes
better, but whose work also contains more inspiration of
the sort to make Freemasons better men, which is after
all the object for which [the] Order exists . . .'. Others
have pointed out that, even though Hutchinson's historical
theories on the origins of the Craft have been rejected
as mere fantasies, 'the book generally elevated the Society

and did much to change it from its notorious, convivial nature to the position it now holds'. More enthusiastic devotees claim that the remarkable development of the ritual and symbolism of the English Craft during this period (i.e. 1770–1813) is largely due to the efforts of writers like Calcott, Hutchinson and Preston. The standard reference works (Kenning, Waite and Mackey) have unstinted praise for Hutchinson's pioneering efforts to raise the moral and intellectual tone of eighteenth-century English Freemasonry by attempting to explain in a rational and scientific manner the true philosophy and moral basis of the Order. Perhaps, it was due largely to early writers like Hutchinson that masonic symbols acquired significances that became enshrined as indispensable features of present-day ritual.

Hutchinson died on 7 April 1814, only three months after the formation of the present United Grand Lodge of England and five days after his beloved wife. They were buried together in the churchyard in Barnard Castle. It is ironic that the grave became vandalized in the 1870s by children. The injury done to the memory of the town's most famous son was railed against in the *Teesdale Mercury*. The brethren of Barnard Lodge were reminded of this scandal and persuaded eventually to raise subscriptions to meet the cost of replacing the damaged tomb with a new stone, suitably engraved. They were not very enthusiastic about this for the work had still not been carried out by 1890. At a meeting of the Durham and Northumberland Architecture and Archaeological Society held in Barnard Castle in 1885, the members were shown the desecrated grave and they reported: 'It is much to be regretted that no memorial in the shape

of a monumental stone marks the place of his interment
. . . Nothing, however, seems to have been done towards
so desirable an object up to the present time, 1890.'
Perhaps the brethren of Barnard Castle remedied that
situation. No matter: Hutchinson had his more lasting
memorials — on the shelves of libraries throughout the
land and in the hearts of Freemasons throughout the
world.

Appendix I

LIST OF HUTCHINSON'S WRITINGS

Note: (1) Those items listed in brackets have not been traced but are referred to in other writings. (2) Those items listed with an asterisk exist only in MS.

(1756	*The Harlot. A Tragedy*)
1757*	*The Parrot and Nightingale. A Fable*
1757*	*The Dog of Quality. A Fable*
1757*	*Hartlepool. A Poem*
1757*	*Poems on Severall Occasions*
1758*	*Baleazar, King of Tyre. A Tragedy* (1st version)
1758–9*	*Honourable Love. In a Series of Letters from Persons in Real Life* (5 vols.)
1760*	*Time. An Introduction*
1760?*	*The Land of Gotham*
1772	*The Hermitage. A British Story* (York: Etherington)
1773	*Doubtful Marriage* (London, 1st edn.); pub. anon.
1773	*An Oration on Masonry Pronounced on . . . 19th June, 1773* (Darlington: J. Sadler; Newcastle: Charnley)
1774	*An Excursion to the Lakes* (London: Wilkie, 1st edn.)

1775   *The Spirit of Masonry* 1st edn. (London: Wilkie and Goldsmith)

(1775   *The Doubtful Marriage. A Narrative drawn from Characters in Real Life*, 1st edn., anon. (London)

1775   *A Week in a Cottage. A Pastoral Tale* (London: Hawes, Clarke and Collins)

1776   *An Excursion to the Lakes* (London: Wilkie), 2nd edn.

1776   *Romance, after the manner of 'The Castle of Otranto'* (London)

1776   *A Week in a Cottage* (London), 2nd edn.

1776   *A View of Northumberland*, 1st vol. (Newcastle: Saint)

(1776   *Poetical Remains* [of his younger brother Robert] (Darlington: Allan))

1778   *An Oration at the Dedication of Freemasons' Hall in Sunderland, 16 July 1778* (London: Baldwin and Humble; Sunderland: Graham)

1778   *A View of Northumberland*, 2nd vol. (Newcastle: Saint)

1779   *An Account of an Ancient Spout, Durham* (Darlington: Allan)

1779   *The State of the Churches in Northumberland* [Hutchinson's edn. of T. Randall's MSS Collection] (Newcastle)

1780   Dutch translation of the Sunderland Oration (Leyden: Koster)

1780   German translation of *The Spirit of Masonry* (Berlin: Stahlbaum)

1781   *Proposals for . . . History of . . . Durham*, 1st edn., June (Darlington: Allan)

1781	*Proposals for . . . History of . . . Durham*, 2nd edn. Dec. (Darlington: Allan)
1782	*Proposals for . . . History of . . . Durham*, 3rd edn. (Darlington: Allan)
1784	*An Address to the Subscribers for the History . . . of . . . Durham* (Darlington: Allan)
1785	*History . . . of Durham . . .* (first 2 vols.) (Newcastle: Hodgson)
1786	*A Recent Case in the Post Office* (Darlington: Allan)
1787*	*The Tears of Bellville Vale. A Poem in Seven Parts*
1788*	*Baleazar. A Tragedy*, 2nd version
1788*	*Pygmalion, King of Tyre. A Tragedy*, [2nd version of *Baleazar*]
1789*	*The Tyrant of Orixo. A Verse Tragedy*
1789	*The Princess of Zanfara* (London: Wilkie and Newcstle: Hodgson), 1st edn., anon.
1792	'An Account of Antiquities in Lancashire', *Archaeologia*, vol. 9
(1792	*Letters Address to the Minister by a Freeholder North of Trent*)
1792	*The Princess of Zanfara* (London: Law and Carlisle: Jollie), 2nd edn.
1792	*The Doubtful Marriage* (London: Law), 2nd edn., anon.
1792	*Notes on the Militia* (Darlington: Allen)
1793	*The Darlington Natural History Society* (Darlington: Allan)
1793	*The Doubtful Marriage* (Dublin), 3rd edn.
1794	*History of Durham*, 3rd vol. (Carlisle: Jollie)
1794	*History . . . of . . . Cumberland*, 2 vols. (Carlisle: Jollie)

1795   *The Spirit of Masonry*, 2nd edn. (Carlisle: Jollie)

1796   *History . . . of . . . Carlisle and its Vicinity* (Carlisle: Jollie)

1800   *The Spirit of Masonry*, 1st American edn. (New York: Collins; Cottom and Stewart)

1802   *The Spirit of Masonry*, 3rd edn. (Carlisle: Jollie)

1809–10   *Letters Relating to the Durham Magistracy* (Newcastle: Hodgson)

1813   *The Spirit of Masonry*, 1st Scottish edn. (Edinburgh: McEwan)

1813   *Grand Order of Masonry Explained* [alternative title of *The Spirit of Masonry*] (Dublin: Charles)

1813   *The Spirit of Masonry*, 2nd Scottish edn. (Edinburgh: McEwan)

1814   *The Spirit of Masonry*, reissue of 3rd edn. (Carlisle: Jollie)

1815   *The Spirit of Masonry* (London: Tegg and Edinburgh: Dick)

(1815   *The Spirit of Masonry*, London: Lewis)

(1815–20?   *The Spirit of Masonry*, London: Badcock)

1823   *History . . . of . . . Durham*, 3 vols, 2nd 4to. edn. (Durham: Walker)

1823   *History . . . of . . . Durham*, 3 vols. 3rd 8vo (pirated) edn.

1843   *The Spirit of Masonry* (London: Spencer)

1855   *The Spirit of Masonry*, reissue of Oliver's edn. (New York: Leonard)

1868   *The Spirit of Masonry*, 2nd reissue of Oliver's edn. (New York: Masonic Publishing and Manufacturing Co.)

1974   *History . . . of . . . Cumberland*, reissue (Wakefield:
              E. P. Publishing Group)

Note: dozens of MSS and printed letters written by and to
Hutchinson have survived. The main collections are:

(1) Newcastle upon Tyne Central Library. MSS L920–H978.
(2) J. Nicholl's *Illustrations of Literature*, vol. 1.
(3) Bodleian Library, Oxford. Don.d. 88; Eng. Misc. d. 149,
     152, 154: Gough, Gen. Top. 43; Eng. Lett. c. 229.

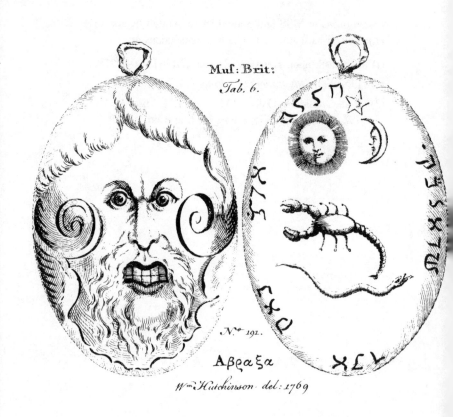

Muſ: Brit:
Tab. 6.

Nᵒ 192.

Αβραξα

Wᵐ Hutchinson del: 1769

Appendix II

THE VARIOUS EDITIONS OF THE SPIRIT OF MASONRY

1775

The Spirit of Masonry
in Moral and Elucidatory Lectures
by William Hutchinson
Master of the Barnard Castle Lodge of Concord
London: J. Wilkie and W. Goldsmith
10½cm × 17½cm
Frontis (engraving of beryl jewel dated 1769)
vii, [1], 237 pgs., 17 pgs, Appendix

1780

Der geist der Maurerey
in moralischen and erlauternden Borlesungen
von Wilhelm Hutchinson
Meister der Barnardcastle loge, Concordia
Berlin: C. 1. Stahlbaum
11cm × 19cm
200 pgs., [1]

1795

The Spirit of Masonry etc. (as for 1775)
by Wm. Hutchinson
The Second Edition

Carlisle: Printed by F. Jollie
MDCCXCV
12½cm × 20½cm
vi, [1], 362 pgs (considerable augmentation of Appendices plus
subscription list)

1800

The Spirit of Masonry etc. (as for 1775)
by Wm. Hutchinson
New York:
Printed by Isaac Collins no. 189 Pearl Street for
Cottom and Stewart, Booksellers and Stationers,
Alexandria
10cm × 17cm
frontis (as for 1775)
[1], vi, [2], 174 pgs., Appendix 22 pgs

1802

The Spirit of Masonry
by Wm. Hutchinson
The Third Edition
with additions
Carlisle: Printed by F. Jollie
10cm × 17½cm
new frontis: (lozenge portrait of WH, by J. Lorres?)
frontis, vi, 359 pgs., [ii]

1813

[Title changed to]
*The Grand Order of Masonry Explained; or the
Virtuous Mason's Companion*
illustrated by several lectures, observations and
charges, etc., etc.,

Dublin: printed by J. Charles, no. 57 Mary Street
10cm × 16½cm
frontis, iv, 212 pgs

1813

[Title as for 1795]
Third Edition
Edinburgh: printed for Samuel McEwan, 21 Abbey Hill
and sold by Andrew Donaldson, Bookseller, Dundee
12cm × 20cm
vi, [1], 336 pgs

1813

[Title as for 1795]
Edinburgh: printed for Samuel McEwan
21 Abbey Hill
(new frontis dated 30 August 1776. G. Nicoll)
frontis, vi, [4], 9–343 pgs

1814

[Title as for 1802]
by Wm. Hutchinson
The Fifth Edition
with Additions
Carlisle: printed by F. Jollie
(frontis and title page portrait as for 1802)
10cm × 18cm
frontis, x, 316 pgs

1815

[Title as for 1775]
by William Hutchinson
Third Edition
London: printed for T. Tegg, 111 Cheapside
and J. Dick, 142 High Street, Edinburgh

(frontis as for 1813 McEwan edn.)
frontis, viii, [1], 343 pgs

1843

[Title as for 1802]
by William Hutchinson, FSA
A new edition with copious notes, critical and explanatory
by the Revd. George Oliver, D.D.
London: Richard Spencer, 314 High Holborn
10cm × 18cm
xvi, 1 × 4 pgs, 45–216 pgs, Appendices [1], 117 pgs, [8 pgs]

1855

[A reissue of the 1843 edn.]
New York: J no. W. Leonard and Co., American masonic
Agency, Clark, Austin and Smith, 3 Park Row
13cm × 21½cm
Collation as for 1843

1866

[Another reissue of the 1843 edn.]
New York: Masonic Publishing and Manufacturing Co.,
432 Broome Street
12½cm × 20cm
Collation as for 1843

Note: according to Wolfstieg (*Bibliographic der Freimaurerischen Literatur*, Leipzig, 1923, vol. 2, p. 93, item no. 21609) there may have been two other, as yet untraced, London editions: one published by Lewis in 1815 and the other by Bodcock in 1815–20.

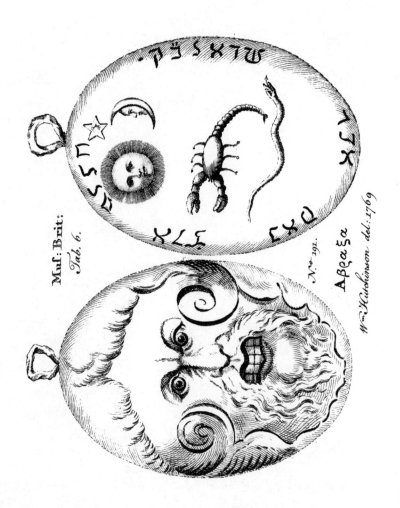

Nᵒ 191.

Aβϛαξα

Wᵐ Hutchinson del: 1769

THE
SPIRIT
of
MASONRY

in
MORAL and *ELUCIDATORY* *LECTURES*.

by Wm HUTCHINSON
MASTER of the Barnardcaſtle Lodge of CONCORD.

— *LONDON* —

Printed for J. WILKIE, N.º 71 in St. Paul's Church-yard
and W. GOLDSMITH, N.º 24 Pater-noſter-Row.

MDCCLXXV.

THE

SANCTION

WHEREAS brother William Hutchinſon has compiled a book, intitled, " The Spirit of Maſonry," and has requeſted our ſanction for the publication thereof; we having peruſed the ſaid book, and finding it will be of uſe to this ſociety, do recommend the ſame.

PETRE, G. M.

ROWLAND HOLT, D. G. M.

THOMAS NOEL, S. G. W.

JOHN HATCH, J. G. W.

ROWLAND BERKLEY, G. T.

JAMES HESELTINE, G. S.

T

(v)

TO THE ANTIENT AND HONOUR-ABLE SOCIETY *of* FREE AND AC-CEPTED MASONS.

BRETHREN,

THE following LECTURES were compofed for the ufe of the LODGE over which I prefided for feveral fuccef-five years. Since that time I have added explanatory notes, to fupport my propo-fitions, or exemplify the principles of the work.

With the utmoft humility and diffi-dence I give thefe LECTURES to the public: they may indeed ferve to detect the wretched artifices ufed by wicked men to impofe upon the world; and if I fucceed fo far with YOU, as to excite the due exercife of thofe moral works which our PROFESSION enjoins, I fhall have my reward.

From the nature of our SOCIETY, and its LAWS, it is difficult to write on the fubject of MASONRY.—We are not

a 2   allowed

allowed that explicit language any other topic would admit of.—My diction will appear technical and abftrufe, to all but MASONS: and with the CRITIC, I am expofed to every degree of feverity; without his candour will admit the MORAL INTENTION of the WORK, in extenuation of thofe imperfections our myftical expreffion throws upon the following pages.

As SUPREME of this SOCIETY, the Right Honourable the LORD PETRE, in the firft place, and after him Mʀ HOLT and the OFFICERS OF THE GRAND LODGE OF ENGLAND, command my moft humble acknowledgments and gratitude, for the candour and condefcention with which this little work was received under their precedency.

MY

MY LORD PETRE,

DEDICATIONS, my Lord, were originally devifed by authors, as fupplications, for protection of their labours, under the illuftrious character to which they were addreffed.

It is for this purpofe, MY LORD, I prefume to prefix your NAME; whilft I confefs myfelf

YOUR LORDSHIP's

MOST DEVOTED,

HUMBLE SERVANT, and

FAITHFUL BROTHER,

W. HUTCHINSON.

THE

CONTENTS.

LECTURES.

LECTURE I.

The DESIGN.

IT is my defign in the following Lectures, to inveftigate the ORDERS OF FREE MASONRY; and under diftinct heads, to arrange my obfervations on the nature of this Society.

On my initiation, I was ftruck with the ceremonials ; and immediately apprehended, there was more conveyed by them, than appeared to the vulgar eye : as I attended to the matter, I was convinced my firft impreffions were juft ; and by my refearches, to difcover their implications, I prefume, I have acquired fome degree of knowledge, touching the

A   Origin

Origin of Mafonry, the reafons of its
feveral inftitutions, the meaning of its
various fymbols, and their import; together with the progrefs of the profeffion.

It is known to the world, but more
particularly to my Brethren, that there
are three degrees of MASONS—AP-
PRENTICES, CRAFTSMEN, and MAS-
TERS—the initiation to, and feveral
advancements from, the order of AP-
PRENTICES, will neceffarily lead my
obfervations to three diftinct channels.

How the feveral myfteries are revealed
to MASONS, they alone know—fo ftead-
faftly have the FRATERNITY preferved their Faith, for many ages, that
this remains a fecret to the world, in
defiance of the corruptions and vices of
Mankind·

In order to comprehend our PRO-
FESSION, we muft look back into the
remoteft antiquity, and from thence col-
lect the feveral parts, which have been
united in the forming of our Order—in
the firft place, we muft give our attention

tion to the Creation of Man, and the ftate of our firft Parent in the Garden of Eden.*

It is not to be doubted, when Adam came from out the hand of his Creator, the Image of God, from whom he immediately proceeded, that he was perfect in Symetry and Beauty; that he was made in the higheft degree of excellence human nature was capable of on earth—calculated for Regions of Felicity and Paradife, where fin or forrow had not known exiftence—made in fuch perfection of body and mind, that he could endure the prefence of God; and was capable of converfing with the Almighty

A 2   face

---

* Genefis—ch. i. ver. 26.
  " And God faid let us make man in our image,
" after our likenefs."
  " Ver. 27.—" So God created man in his own
" image, in the image of God created he him."
  Ver. 31.—" And God faw every thing that he
" had made, and behold it was very good."
  Ch. 2. ver. 7.—" And the Lord God formed
" the man of the duft of the ground, and breathed
" into his noftrils the breath of life; and man
" became a living foul."

face to face*—fo much was he fuperior
to the chofen ones of Ifrael.—He was
endowed with underftanding fuitable to
his ftation, as one whom the Almighty
deigned to vifit; and his heart was poffeffed of all the VIRTUES unpolluted:
endowments of an heavenly temper—
his hours were full of wifdom, exulta-
tion, and tranfport—the Book of Nature
was revealed to his comprehenfion, and
all her myfteries were open to his underftanding—he knew whence and what
he was.—Even this was but a minute
degree of his capacity; for aftonifhing
as it may appear to us, yet it is an
uncontrovertable truth, that he had a
competent knowledge of the mighty,
the tremendous CREATOR OF THE
UNIVERSE;—he faw him with his
natural eyes, he heard his voice, he underftood his laws, and was prefent to his
Majefty.

To this fountain of human perfection
and wifdom, we muft neceffarily look
back,

* Genefis, ch. ii. ver. 16—17—19.—Ch. iii.
ver. 9—10—11—12—17.

back, for all the science and learning which blessed the earliest ages of the world—calculated for such exalted felicity and elevated enjoyments, placed in regions of peace, where Angels miniſtred and the Divinity walked abroad, was the parent of mankind.

But alas he fell!—his diſobedience forfeited all that glory and felicity—and horrible to recount, even in the midſt of this exalted ſtate, SATAN prevailed!

If we preſume to eſtimate the change which befel ADAM, on his expulſion from Paradiſe, by the deformity that took place on the face of the world, we ſhould be apt to believe the exile, though not diſtorted in body, was yet darkened in underſtanding—inſtead of confidence and ſteady faith, that diſtruſt and jealouſy would take place, and diſbelief confound even teſtimony; that argument would be deprived of definition, and wander by excentric propoſitions; that confuſion would uſurp the throne of wiſdom, and folly of judgment; thorns and thiſtles grow up in the place of thoſe excellent

A 3   flowers

flowers of science which flourished in Eden, and darkness cloud the day of his capacity.

It is not possible for me to determine, from any evidence given to us, in what degree disobedience and sin immediately contracted the understanding of ADAM; but we are certain that great and dreadful effects very early took place on Adam's posterity.—We may conclude, memory was retained by our first parent in all its energy—a terrible portion of the punishment his disobedience had incurred; restoring to him perfect images, and never-dying estimates, of what he had lost, and thereby increasing the bitterness of what he had purchased. Through the endowments of memory, ADAM would necessarily teach to his family the sciences which he had comprehended in Eden, and the knowledge he had gained of NATURE and her GOD.—It will follow, that some of them would retain those lessons of wisdom, and faithfully transmit them to posterity.—No doubt the family of Cain (who bore the seal

of

of the curfe on his forehead) was given up to ignorance.*

Tradition would deliver down the doctrines of our firft parents with the utmoft truth and certainty, whilft the Antideluvians enjoyed that longivity of which the books of Mofes give evidence—but when men came to multiply exceedingly upon the face of the earth, and were difperfed to the diftant regions of the globe, then the ineftimable leffons of KNOWLEDGE and TRUTH, taught by the firft men, fell into confufion and corruption, and were retained pure and in perfection but by few —— thofe few, to our great confolation, have handed them down to after ages—they alfo retained the UNIVERSAL LANGUAGE, uncorrupted, with the confufion of the plains of Shinar, and preferved it to pofterity.

Thus we muft neceffarily look back to OUR FIRST PARENT, as the original Profeffor of the WORSHIP OF THE TRUE GOD, to whom the Religion and

A 4

myfteries

---

* Genefis, cha. iv ver. 16.—" And Cain went " out from the prefence of the Lord."

myfteries of NATURE were firft revealed, and from whom all the WISDOM of
the world was in the beginning derived.

In thofe times, when the prefent Rules
and maxims of our profeffion of FREE
MASONRY had their beginning, the
minds of men were poffeffed of Allego-
ries, Emblems, and myftic devices, in
which, peculiar fciences, manners, inftitutions, and doctrines in many nations
were wrapt up—this was an invention of
the earlieft ages—the priefts in Egypt fe-
creted the myfteries of their religion from
the vulgar, by fymbols and hieroglyphics
comprehenfible alone to thofe of their
own order. The priefts of Rome and
Greece practifed other fubtleties by which
the art of divination was enveiled, and
their oracles were intelligible only to
their brethren, who expounded them to
the people.

Thefe examples were WISELY adopted
for the purpofes of concealing the myfteries of MASONRY—like the Cybil's
leaves, the fecrets of the brotherhood
would appear to the world as indiftinct
                                         and

and fcattered fragments, whilft they convey to MASONS an uniform and well-connected fyftem.

In the forming of this fociety, which is at once RELIGIOUS AND CIVIL, great regard has been given to the firft knowledge of the GOD OF NATURE, and that acceptable fervice wherewith he is well pleafed.

This was the firft ftage on which our originals thought it expedient to place the foundation of MASONRY:—they had experienced that from religion all civil ties and obligations were compacted, and that thence proceeded all the bonds which could unite mankind in focial intercourfe:—hence it was that they laid the corner ftone of the EDIFICE on the bofom of religion.*

In

---

* " *Religions* all! defcending from the fkies
" To wretched man, the goddefs in her left
" Holds out this world, and, in her right, the next:
" *Religion!* the fole-voucher man is man;
" Sup-

In the earlieft ages, after the deluge,
in thofe nations made known to us, the
fervice of the true God was clouded with
imagery, and defiled by idolatry.—Men
who had not been taught the doctrines
of truth, by thofe who retained the wifdom of the Antideluvians, but were left
to the operations of their own judg-
ments, perceived that there was fome
great caufe of nature's uniformity, and
wonderful progreffions of her works :
fuitable to their ignorance, they reprefented the Author of thofe works, by
fuch objects as ftruck their obfervation,
for their powerful effects on the face of
the world—from whence the SUN AND
MOON

" Supporter fole of man above himfelf;
" Ev'n in this night of frailty, change, and death,
" She gives the foul a foul that acts a *God.*
" *Religion! Providence! an after ftate!*
" *Here* is firm footing; here is folid rock ;
" This can fupport us; all is fea befides;
" Sinks under us ; beftorms, and then devours.
" His hand the good man faftens on the fkies,
" And bids earth roll, nor feels her idle whirl.

Young's Night Thoughts.

MOON became the symbols of the Deity.*

MOSES

---

* The posterity of *Ham* forsook the doctrines of their predecessor, for the Deity whose adoration he taught, they soon substituted the symbol, and for the original, worshipped the *Sun*, which was regarded in the first ages after the deluge, as the *Type* or *Emblem* of the *Divinity*.

" The descendants of *Chus*, called *Cuthites*, " were those Emigrants who carried their rites, " religions, and customs into various quarters of " the globe;—they were the first apostates from " the *Truth*, yet great in worldly wisdom;—they " were joined in their expeditions by other nations, " especially by the collateral branches of their " family, the *Mizraim, Caphtorim*, and the sons " of *Canaan*;—these were all of the line of *Ham*, " who was held by his posteritie in the highest " veneration;—they called him *Amon*, and hav- " in process of time raised him to a Divinity, they " worshipped him as the *Sun*, and from this wor- " ship they were stiled *Amonians*."

" The Deitie which they worshipped was the " *Sun*, but they soon conferred his titles upon " some of their ancestors; whence arose a mixed " worship. They particularly deified the great " Patriarch who was the head of their line, and " worshipped him as the *Fountain of Light*; ma- " king the *Sun* only an emblem of his influence " and power."

Bryant's Analysis of ancient Mythology.

MOSES was learned in all the wifdom of the Egyptians ; he was initiated in all the knowledge of the WISEMEN of that nation, by whom the learning of antiquity had been retained and held facred ; wrapped up from the eye of the wicked and vulgar, in fymbols and hieroglyphics, and communicated to men of their own order only, with care, fecrecy, and circumfpection.—This fecrecy is not in any wife to be wondered at, when we confider the perfecution which would have followed a faith unacceptable to the ignorance of the nations who were enveloped in fuperftition and bigotry ; and more particularly, as thefe fages were in poffeffion of that valuable knowledge of the powers of nature, of the qualities of matter, and properties of things, fo dangerous to be communicated to wicked and ignorant men, from whofe malevolence the moft horrid offences might be derived : of which we may judge by the extraordinary and aftonifhing performances even of thofe impious and unenlightened men, who contended with

MOSES

MOSES, in the miracles he performed, under the immediate impreffion and influence of the Deity.*

MOSES divefted the worfhip of the Deity of its cloak of myfteries and images, and taught the Jews the knowledge of the God of the Univerfe, unpolluted with the errors of the nations of the earth, and uncorrupted with the devices and ludicrous ceremonies inftituted by the people of the Eaft, from whom he derived his firft comprehenfion and knowledge of the Divinity.†

The

---

* Exodus, ch. vii. ver. 11—12—22. Ch. viii. ver. 7—18.

† The Author of " the Differtation on the an-
" tient Pagan Myfteries," defending Dr Warburton's pofitions againft Dr Leland, writes thus :
" that to the *Pagan Divinity* there was not only
" an open and public worfhip, but alfo a fecret
" worfhip paid to them, to which none were ad-
" mitted but thofe who had been felected by pre-
" paratory ceremonies, called *Initiation*. This
" fecret worfhip was termed the *Myfteries*."

" Of thefe there were two forts, the *greater*
" and the *leffer* : according to the Bifhop of Glou-
" cefter,

14   The D E S I G N.

The second ſtage of FREE MASONRY
is grounded on this period—the TEM-
PLE AT JERUSALEM owns the probation of the CRAFTSMEN.

Moſes

" ceſter, the leſſer taught, by certain ſecret rites
" and ſhews, the *Origin* of *Society*, and the doc-
" trine of a *future State*; they were *preparatory* to
" the *greater*, and might be ſafely communicated
" to all the *initiated*, without exception.

" The *Arcana of the greater Myſteries*, were the
" doctrine of the *Unity*, and the detection of the
" errors of the vulgar *Polytheiſm*; theſe were not
" communicated to all the aſpirants, without ex-
" ception, but only to a ſmall and *ſelect number*,
" who were judged capable of the *ſecret*."

" The initiated were obliged by the moſt *ſolemn*
" *engageme ts*, to commence a life of ſtricteſt piety
" and virtue; it was proper therefore to give them
" all the encouragement and aſſiſtance neceſſary
" for this purpoſe Now in the Pagan world
" there was a powerful temptation to vice and
" debauchery, the profligate examples of their
" Gods. Ego homuncio hoc non facerem, was
" the abſolving formula, whenever any one was
" reſolved to give a looſe to his paſſions. This
" evil the *Myſteries* remedied, by ſtriking at the
" root of it; therefore ſuch of the *initiated* as
                                    " were

Moſes was alſo poſſeſſed of knowledge
ſuperior to that of his Egyptian teachers,
through the revelations and inſpirations
of the Deity;—he had acquired the com-
prehenſion of, and was inſtructed to decipher all the hieroglyphical characters
uſed

" were judged capable, were made acquainted
" with the whole deluſion. The *Myſtagogue* taught
" them, that Jupiter, Mercury, Bacchus, Venus,
" Mars, and the whole rabble of licentious Dei-
" ties, were only dead mortals ; ſubject, in life,
" to the ſame paſſions and infirmities with them-
" ſelves ; but having been on other accounts
" benefactors to mankind, grateful poſteritie had
" deified them ; and with their virtues, had in-
" diſcreetly canonized their vices.

" The fabulous *Gods* being thus rooted, the
" *Supreme Cauſe of all things* naturally took their
" place. Him they were taught to conſider, as
" the *Creator* of the univerſe, who pervaded all
" things by his virtue, and governed all by his
" providence. But here it muſt be obſerved, that
" the diſcovery of this *Supreme Cauſe*, was ſo
" made, as to be conſiſtent with the notion of
" local tutelary deities, beings ſuperior to men,
" and inferior to God, and by him ſet over the
" ſeveral parts of his creation. This was an
" opinion univerſally holden by antiquity, and
                                          " never

ufed by that people in their records:—it was no doubt a part of the original knowledge, to exprefs by characters to the eye, the thoughts and fentiments of the mind —but this was obfcured and debafed in after ages by fymbols and hieroglyphics: yet by the immediate difpenfation of heaven, Mofes attained the knowledge of thofe original characters ; by which he was enabled to reveal to his people, and preferve to pofterity, the COMMANDMENTS OF GOD, delivered to him on the

---

" never brought into queftion by any Theift. " What the *Arcana* of the *Myfteries* overthrew, " was the vulgar *Polytheifm*, the worfhip of dead " men.

" It was natural for thefe politicians, to keep " this a fecret in the *Myfteries* ; for in their opi- " nion, not only the extinction, but even the gra- " dation of their falfe gods, would have too " much difconcerted and embroiled the eftablifhed " fyftem of vulgar *Polytheifm*."

From hence we may be led to determine, that to Mofes the fecret of the *Egyptian Mythology* was divulged by his preceptors, and the knowledge of the *only God* revealed to him, divefted of all the *fymbols and devices* which engaged the *vulgar*.

the mount by infcribing them on tables
of ftone.*

It is natural to conceive that the Ifraelites would be inftructed in this act, by
which the will of the Deity was communicated;—they would be led to write the
doctrines of their leader, and his expo-
fitions of the law, that they fhould be
preferved to their children;—and if we
give credit to the obfervations and conjectures of learned travellers, the written
mountains remain monuments of the pe-
regrinating Hebrews to this day.

B   But

---

* Exodus, ch. xxxi. ver. 18.—" And he gave
" unto Mofes, when he had made an end of com-
" muning with him upon Mount Sinai, two ta-
" bles of teftimony, tables of ftone, *written* with
" the finger of God."

Ch. xxxiv. ver. 1.—" And the Lord faid unto
" Mofes, hew thee two tables of ftone like unto
" the firft, and I will *write upon thefe tables* the
" words that were in the firft tables, which thou
" brakeft."

Ver. 27.—" And the Lord faid unto Mofes,
" *write thou thefe words*; for after the tenor of
" thefe words I have made a covenant with thee
" and with Ifrael."

But to return to the progreſſions of our profeſſion.—It is not to be preſumed, that we are a ſet of men, profeſſing religious principles contrary to the revelations and doctrines of the SON OF GOD, reverencing a Deity by the denomination of the GOD OF NATURE, and denying that mediation which is graciouſly offered to all true believers.—The members of OUR SOCIETY at this day, in the third ſtage of maſonry, confeſs themſelves to be CHRISTIANS—" the " veil of the temple is rent—the builder " is ſmitten—and we are raiſed from the " tomb of tranſgreſſion."

I humbly preſume, it is not to be underſtood, that the name of MASON, in this ſociety, denotes that the origin or riſe of ſuch ſociety was ſolely from builders, architects, or mechanics:—at the times in which MOSES ordained the ſetting up of the ſanctuary,* and when SOLO-

---

* Exodus, ch. xxxi. ver. 2.—" See, I have called " by name, Bezaleel, the ſon of Uri, the ſon of " Hur, of the tribe of Judah."

Ver

SOLOMON was about to build the
TEMPLE at Jerufalem, they felected
from out the people, thofe men who were
enlightened with the true faith, and being full of wifdom and religious fervor,
were found proper to conduct thefe

B 2   works

Ver. 3.—" And I have filled him with the fpirit
" of God, in wifdom, and in underftanding, and
" in knowledge, and in all manner of workman-
" fhip."

Ver. 4.—" To devife cunning works, to work
" in gold, and in filver, and in brafs."

Ver. 5.—" And in cutting of ftones to fet them,
" and in carving of timber, to work in all manner
" of workmanfhip."

Ver 6.—" And in the hearts of all that are wife-
" hearted I have put wifdom, that they may make
" all that I have commanded thee."

Ver. 7.—" The tabernacle of the congregation,
" &c."

Ch. xxxvi. ver. 1.—" Then wrought Bezaleel
" and Aholiab, and every wife-hearted man, in
" whom the Lord put wifdom and underftanding,
" to know how to work all manner of work for
" the fervice of the fanctuary, according to all
" that the Lord had commanded."

Ver. 2.—" And Mofes called Bezaleel and Aho-
" liab, and every wife-hearted man, in whofe
" heart the Lord had put wifdom, even every
" one whofe heart ftirred him up to come unto
" the Work to do it."

works of piety.—It was on thofe occafions that our predeceffors appeared to
the world as architects, and were formed
into a body, under falutary rules, for the
government of thofe who were employed
in thefe great works: fince which period
builders have adopted the name of mafons, as an honourary diftinction and title
to their profeffion.—I am induced to believe the name of MASON has its derivation from a language, in which it implies fome ftrong indication, or diftinction,
of the nature of the fociety; and that it
has not its relation to architects.—The
French word MASON fignifies a Family
or particular race of people:—it feems as
if the name was compounded of Μαω-
Σωκν, QUERO SALVUM; and the title
of MASONRY no more than a corruption
of Μεσυρανεω, SUM IN MEDIO COELI,
or Μαζυςοοθ, SIGNA COELESTIA.
Job xxxviii. 32.—which conjecture is
ftrengthened by our fymbols.*

I am

---

* The titles of mafons and mafonry moft probably were derived from the greek language, as
the greek idiom is adopted by them, and is fhewn
in

I am inclined to determine, that the appellation of MASON implies a member of a RELIGIOUS SECT, and a profeſſed devotee of the Deity, " WHO IS SEATED " IN THE CENTRE OF HEAVEN."

To prove theſe ſeveral propoſitions in MASONRY to be true, and to demon-ſtrate to MASONS the importance of their order, ſhall be the ſubject of the following lectures.

The principles of MORALITY are rigorouſly enjoined us; — CHARITY
B 3

AND

---

in many inſtances in the courſe of this work—the Druids, when they committed any thing to wri-ting, uſed the greek alphabet—and I am bold to aſſert, the moſt perfect remains of the Druids rites and ceremonies are preſerved in the ceremo-nials of maſons, that are to be found exiſting among mankind.—My brethren may be able to trace them with greater exactneſs than I am at liberty to explain to the public.—The original names of maſons and maſonry may probably be derived from, or corrupted of Μυςήριον, res arcana, myſteries, and Μύρης, ſacris initiatus myſta—thoſe initiated to ſacred myſteries.

AND BROTHERLY LOVE are our in-indifpenfable duty:—How they are pre-fcribed to us, and their practice enforced, will alfo be treated of in the following pages.

My original defign in thefe lectures, was not only to explain to my brethren the nature of their profeffion, but alfo to teftify to the world, that our MYSTE-RIES are important; and to take away the reproach which hath fallen upon this fociety, by the vices, ignorance, or irre-gularities of fome profligate men, who have been found among MASONS.—Should the errors of a few, ftain and render ignominious a whole fociety, or bring infamy and contempt on a body of men; there is no affociation on earth, either civil or religious, which might not be affected.

LEC-

LECTURE II.

On the Rites, Ceremonies, *and* Inftitutions *of the* Antients.

THERE is no doubt that our ceremonies and myfteries were derived from the rites, ceremonies, and inftitutions of the antients, and fome of them from the remoteft ages. Our morality is deduced from the maxims of the Grecian philofophers, and perfected by the chriftian revelation.

The inftitutors of this fociety had their eyes on the progreffion of religion, and they fymbolized it, as well in the firft ftage, as in the advancement of mafons.—The knowledge of the God of

B 4   Nature

Nature forms the firſt eſtate of our profeſſion ; the worſhip of the Deity under
the jewiſh law, is deſcribed in the ſecond ſtage of maſonry ; and the chriſtian
diſpenſation is diſtinguiſhed in the laſt
and higheſt order.

It is extremely difficult, with any degree of certainty, to trace the exact origin
of our ſymbols, or from whence our ceremonies or myſteries were particularly
derived.—I ſhall point out ſome antient
inſtitutions from whence they may have
been deduced.

The ASSIDEANS (a ſect among the
Jews, divided into חסידים the merci-
ful, and צדיקים the juſt) the fathers
and predeceſſors of the PHARISEES and
ESSENES:—they preferred their traditions before the written word, and ſet up
for a ſanctity and purity that exceeded
the law: they at laſt fell into the error
of the Sadduces, in denying the reſur-
rection, and the faith of rewards and puniſhments after this life.

The

The ESSENES* were of very remote antiquity, ànd it hath been argued by divines, that they were as antient as the de-

---

* " The etymologies of the names Eſſæi or
" Eſſeni, i. e. *Eſſenes*, are divers; that which I
" prefer is from the Syriac ‫אסא‬ Aſa, ſigni-
" fying Θεραπεύειν, to heal or cure diſeaſes; for
" though they gave themſelves chiefly to the ſtudy
" of the Bible, yet with all they ſtudied phyſic."
    " Concerning the beginning of this ſect, from
" whom or when it began, it is hard to deter-
" mine. Some make them as antient as the Re-
" chabites, and the Rechabites to have differed
" only in the addition of ſome rules and ordi-
" nances from the Kenites, mentioned Judg. i. 16.
" and thus by conſequence the Eſſenes were as
" antient as the Iſraelites departure out of Egypt:
" for Jethro, Moſes's father-in law, as appears
" by the text, was a Kenite: but neither of theſe
" ſeemeth probable, for the Kenites are not men-
" tioned in ſcripture, as a diſtinct order or ſect of
" people, but as a diſtinct family, kindred, or na-
" tion. Numb. xxiv. 2.—Secondly, the Rechabites
" did not build houſes, but dwelt in tents; nei-
" ther did they deal in huſbandry; they ſowed
" no ſeed, nor planted vine-yards, nor had any.
" Jer. lv. 7.—The *Eſſenes*, on the contrary, dwelt
" not in tents, but in houſes, and they employed
" themſelves eſpecially in huſbandry. One of the
Hebrew

departure of the ISRAELITES out of EGYPT. They might take their rife, from that difperfion of their nation, which hap-

---

" Hebrew doctors faith, that the *Effenes* were Na-
" zarites: but that cannot be, becaufe the law
" enjoined the Nazarites, when the time of the
" confecration was on, to prefent themfelves at
" the door of the tabernacle or temple. Numb. vi.
" Now the *Effenes* had no accefs to the temple;
" when, therefore, or from what author this fect
" took its beginning is uncertain. The firft
" that I find mentioned by the name of an *Effene*
" Jofephus, l. xiii. c. 19.) was one Judas, who
" lived in the time of Ariftobulus, the fon of
" Jannes Hyrcanus, before our Saviour's birth
" about one hundred years: however this fect was
" of greater antiquity, for all three, pharifees,
" Sadduces, and *Effenes*, were in Jonathan's time,
" the brother of Judas Maccabeus, who was fifty
" years before Ariftobulus. Certain it is, that this
" fect continued until the days of our Saviour and
" after: Philo and Jofephus fpeak of them as liv-
" ing in their times. What might be the reafon
" then, that there is no mention of them in the
" New Teftament? I anfwer, firft, the number
" of them feemeth not to have been great in Philo
" and Jofephus's time, about four thoufand, which
" being difperfed in many cities, made the faction
" weak: and happily in Jerufalem, when our Sa-
" viour lived, they were either few or none. Se-
           " condly,

happened after their being carried captive into Babylon. The principal character of this sect was, that they chose retirement,

---

" condly, if we obferve hiftories, we fhall find
" them peaceable and quiet, not oppofing any,
" and therefore not fo liable to reproof as the
" Pharifees and Sadduces, who oppofed each
" other, and both joined againft Chrift. Thirdly,
" why might they not as well be paffed over in
" filence in the New Teftament (efpecially con-
" taining themfelves quietly without contradiction
" of others) as the Rechabites in the Old Tefta-
" ment, of whom there is mention only once, and
" that obliquely, although their order continued
" about three hundred years before this teftimony
" was given of them by the prophet Jeremy; for
" between John (with whom Jonadab was coeta-
" nean) and Zedekia, chronologers obferve the
" diftance of many years. Laftly, though the
" name of *Effenes* be not found in fcripture, yet
" we fhall find in St Paul's Epiftles many things
" reproved, which were taught in the fchool of
" the *Effenes :* of this nature was that advice
" given to Timothy, 1 Tim. v. 13. Drink no
" longer water, but ufe a little wine.—Again,
" 1 Tim. iv. 3. Forbidding to marry, and com-
" manding to abftain from meat, is a doctrine of
" devils—but efpecially Coloff. 2d, in many paf-
" fages the apoftle feemeth directly to point at
" them: Let no man condemn you in meat and
                                        " drink,

ment, were fober, were induftrious; had
all things in common; paid the higheft
regard to the moral precepts of the law,
but neglected the ceremonial, any further
than

" drink, v. 16.—Let no man bear rule over you,
" by humblenefs of mind, and worfhipping of
" angels, v. 18.—τὸ δοϲμαϊιζεϑε, why are ye fub-
" ject to ordinances, v. 20.—The apoftle ufeth
" the word δοϲμαϊα, which was applied by the
" Effenes to denote their *ordinances, aphorifms,*
" *or conftitutions.*—In the verfe following he gives
" an inftance of fome particulars, Touch not,
" tafte not, handle not, ver. 21.—Now the junior
" company of Effenes might not touch their fe-
" niors : and in their diet, their tafte was limited
" to bread, falt, water, and hyffop : and thefe
" ordinances they undertook, δια ποοϑον σοφιας,
" faith Philo, for the love of *wifdom* : but the
" apoftle concludeth, ver. 23. that thefe things
" had only λόγον σοφίας a fhew of wifdom. And
" whereas Philo termeth the religion of the Effenes
" by the name of ϑεραπεία, which word fignifieth
" religious worfhip, the apoftle termeth in the
" fame verfe, εθελοθρησκειαν, voluntary religion,
" or will worfhip : yea, where he termeth their
" doctrine παϊρίαν φιδοσοφίαν, a kind of philofophy
" received from their forefathers by tradition, St
" Paul biddeth them beware of philofophy, ver. 8."
                    Godwyn's Mofes and Aaron.

than what regarded bodily cleanlinefs, the obfervation of the fabbath, and making an annual prefent to THE TEMPLE AT JERUSALEM. They never affociated with women, nor admitted them into their retreats. By the moft SACRED OATHS, though they were in general averfe to fwearing, or to requiring an oath, they bound all whom they INITIATED among them, to the obfervance of piety, juftice, fidelity, and modefty; to conceal the fecrets of the fraternity, preferve the books of their inftructors, and with great care commemorate the names of the angels. They held, that GOD was furrounded by fpiritual beings, who were MEDIATORS with him, and and therefore to be reverenced. Second, that the foul is defiled by the body, and that all bodily pleafures hurt the foul, which they believed to be immortal, though they denied the refurrection of the body, as it would return the foul to fin. Third, that there was a great MYSTERY in numbers, particularly in the number SEVEN; they therefore attributed a natural holinefs to the feventh or SABBATH DAY, which they ob-

ferved

ferved more ftrictly than the other Jews.
They fpent their time moftly in contemplation, and abftained from every gratifi-
cation of the fenfes. The ESSENES introduced their maxims into the CHRIS-
TIAN CHURCH; and it is alledged by
the learned, that St PAUL, in his epiftles
to the Ephefians and Coloffians, particularly cenfures the tenets of this fect.

     " Of thefe ESSENES there were two
" forts; fome were THEORICKS, giv-
" ing themfelves wholly to fpeculation;
" others P R A C T I C K S, laborious and
" painful in the daily exercife of thofe
" arts or manufactories in which they
" were moft fkilful. Of the latter, Philo
" treateth in his book, intituled, Quod
" omnis vir probus : of the former, in
" the book following, intituled, De vita
" contemplativa."—Godwyn's Mofes and
Aaron.

     The ESSENES were denied accefs to
the TEMPLE.

     The PRACTICKS and THEORICKS
both agreed in their aphorifms or ordi-
                     nances;

nances; but in certain circumstances they differed.

1. The PRACTICKS dwelt in the cities; the THEORICKS shunned the cities, and dwelt in gardens and solitary villages.

2. The PRACTICKS spent the day in manuel crafts, keeping of sheep, looking to bees, tilling of ground, &c. they were artificers. The THEORICKS spent the day in meditation and prayer; whence they were, from a kind of excellency, by Philo, termed supplicants.

3. The PRACTICKS had every day their dinner and supper allowed them; the THEORICKS only their supper.

The PRACTICKS had for their commons, every one his dish of water-gruel and bread; the THEORICKS only bread and salt: if any were of a more delicate palate than other, to him it was permitted to eat hyssop; their drink for both was common water.

Some

Some are of opinion that thefe THEO-
RICKS were CHRISTIAN MONKS; but
the contrary appeareth for thefe reafons.

1. In the whole book of Philo, concerning the Theoricks, there is no mention either of Chrift or Chriftians, of the
Evangelifts or Apoftles.

2. The THEORICKS, in that book of
Philo's, are not any new fect of late beginning, as the chriftians at that time
were, as is clearly evinced by Philo's
own words, in calling the doctrine of the
ESSENES πάτριαν φιλοσοφιαν, a philofophy
derived unto them by tradition from their
forefathers.

In Grecian antiquity, we find a feftival
celebrated in honour of CÆRES,* at
Eleufis,

---

* " It was the moft celebrated and myfterious
" folemnity of any in Greece ; whence it is often
" called, by way of eminence, the *Myfteries*; and
" fo fuperftitioufly careful were they to conceal
" the *facred rites*, that if any perfon divulged any
" of them, he was thought to have called down
" fome

Eleufis, a town of Attica, where the
Athenians, with great pomp and many
ceremonies, attended the myftic rites.——
Hiftorians tell us, that thefe rites were a
MYSTICAL reprefentation of what the
mythologifts taught of that goddefs; and
were of fo facred a nature, that no lefs
than death was the penalty of difcovery.

C   There

" fome divine judgment upon his head, and it was
" accounted unfafe to abide in the fame houfe
" with him; wherefore he was apprehended as a
" public offender, and fuffered death. Such alfo
" was the fecrecy of thefe *rites*, that if any per-
" fon, who was not lawfully initiated, did but
" out of ignorance or miftake, chance to be pre-
" fent at the myfterious rites, he was put to death.
" The neglect of initiation was looked upon as a
" crime of a very heinous nature ; infomuch that
" it was one part of the accufation for which
" *Socrates* was condemned to death.   Perfons
" convicted of witchcraft, or any other heinous
" crime, or had committed murder, though in-
" voluntary, were debarred from thefe myfteries.
" In later times certain inftitutions were made,
" called the leffer myfteries, and were ufed as
" preparative to the greater; for no perfons were
" initiated in the greater, unlefs they had purified
at

There was another great festival celebrated by the Greeks at PLATÆA, in
honour of JUPITER ELEUTHERIUS;
the

" at the lesser. The persons who were to be ad-
" mitted to the greater mysteries, made their sa-
" crifice a year after purification, the secret rites
" of which (some few excepted to which only
" priests were conscious) were frankly revealed to
" them.—The manner of *initiation* was thus: the
" candidates being crowned with myrtle, had ad-
" mittance by night into a place called Μυσικω
" σηκος, *i.e.* the *mystical temple*, which was an
" edifice so vast and capacious, that the most am-
" ple theatre did scarce exceed it. At their en-
" trance they purified themselves by washing their
" hands in holy water, and at the same time were
" admonished to present themselves with minds
" pure and undefiled, without which the external
" cleanness of the body would by no means be
" accepted. After this the *holy mysteries* were
" read to them out of a book called Πετρωμα,
" which word is derived from πετρα a stone; be-
" cause the book was nothing else but two stones
" fitly cemented together. Then the priest that
" initiated them, called Ιεροφαντης, proposed cer-
" tain questions, to which they returned answers
" in *a set form*, as may be seen in Meursius's Trea-
" tise on this festival. This done, strange and
                                        " amazing

the affembly was compofed of delegates
from almoft all the cities of GREECE ;
and the rites which were inftituted in
honour of JUPITER, as the guardian of
C 2   LI

" amazing objects prefented themfelves ; fometimes
" the place they were in feemed to fhake round
" them, fometimes appeared bright and refplen-
" dent with light and radiant fire ; and then again
" covered with black darknefs and horror—fome-
" times thunder and lightning, fometimes frightful
" noifes and bellowings, fometimes terrible appa
" ritions aftonifhed the trembling fpectators. The
" *garments* in which they were *initiated* were ac-
" counted *facred*, and of no lefs efficacy to avert
" evils than charms and incantations.

   " The chief perfon that attended at the initia-
" tion, was called Ιεροφαντης, i. e. *a revealer of*
" *holy things.* The hierophantes had three affift-
" tants, the firft of which was called from his
" office Δαδοδχος, i. e. *torch-bearer ;* the fecond
" was called Κῆρυξ, or *the cryer* ; the third mini-
" ftred at the altar, and was for that reafon
" named Ο'δπὶ Βωμῶ.

   " *Hierophantes* is faid to have been a *type* of the
" *great Creator of all things,*

   " Διαδοδχος of the *Sun,*
   " Κῆρυξ of *Mercury,*
   " And Ο'δπὶ τῶ Βωμῶ of the *Moon.*"

LIBERTY, were performed with the ut-
moſt magnificence and ſolemn pomp.

In BALSARA, and along the banks
of JORDAN, a ſect of chriſtians are
known, who call themſelves CHRIS-
TIANS OF St. JOHN; but as they profeſs no knowledge of the union of the
third perſon in the TRINITY, I am induced to believe no part of our profeſſion
was derived from them. Their ceremonies and myſteries are founded on traditions, and they permit no canonical book
to be received amongſt them.

In the inſtitution of the orders of
KNIGHTHOOD, the eyes of the founders were fixed on various religious ceremonies, being the general mode of
antient times — Knights of the Bath had
their hair cut and beards ſhaven, were
ſhut up in the chapel alone all the night
preceding their initiation, there to ſpend
the ſolemn hours in faſting, meditation,
and prayer: they offered their ſword at
the altar, as devotees to the will of heaven, and aſſumed a motto expreſſive of
                                        their

their vow, " Tres in Uno;" meaning the unity of the three theological virtues — Various orders of Knights wear a crofs on their cloaks: the order of Chrift, in Livonia, inftituted in 1205, wore this enfign, and were denominated brothers of the fword.—The order of the Holy Ghoft wear a golden crofs.

An antient writing which is preferved amongft mafons with great refpect, requires my attention in this place, as it difcovers to us what the antient mafons regarded as the foundation of our profeffion [*See the Appendix*].

This writing is faid to have come from the hand of King Henry the Sixth, who began his reign in 1422: it is in the form of an inquifition for the difcovery of the nature of mafonry.

From this antient record we are told, " that the myftery of mafonry is a " knowledge of nature and its opera- " tions." [*Appendix*].

C 3   " That

" That this fcience arofe in the Eaft."*
—From the Eaft, it is well known, learning firft extended itfelf into the weftern
world, and advanced into Europe.—The
Eaft was an expreffion ufed by the antients to imply Chrift:—in this fenfe we
find Ανατοαη ufed in the prophets.

" That the Phœnicians firft introduced
" this fcience."† [*Appendix*].

" That

---

* Ezekiel, ch. xliii. ver. 2.
" And behold the glory of the God of Ifrael
" came from the way of the Eaft : and his voice
" was like the noife of many waters, and the earth
" fhined with his glory."
Ch. xxiv. ver. 2.—" The Eaft gate fhall be fhut,
" it fhall not be opened, and no man fhall enter
" in by it, becaufe the glory of the God of Ifrael
" hath entered in by it, therefore it fhall be fhut."
Ver 3.—" It is for the Prince. The Prince
" he fhall fit in it to eat bread before the Lord."

† It is the opinion of many great antiquaries,
that the Druids were eftablifhed in Britain before
they gained any footing in Gaul:—to quote the
authorities for this, would render my work too
prolix.

In

" That Pythagoras journey'd into
" Egypt and Syria, and brought with
" him thefe myſteries into Greece."
[*Appendix*].

It is known to all the learned that
Pythagoras travelled into Egypt, and
was initiated there into feveral different
C 4   orders

In order to ſhew how early the maxims and
principles of the eaſtern nations might be communicated to this land, I muſt mention ſome obſer-
vations of learned men.

Arthur Agard, Deputy Chamberlain of the
Exchequer, 1570, (vide Bibl. Cotton. Fauſtina,
E. V.) ſpeaking of the admeaſurement of lands in
this country, ſays, " Our nation having their
" origin from the Trojans, brought from thence
" the ſame order as was obſerved in that country,
" our lands were meaſured by hides, the etymo-
" logy whereof is derived from Dido's act men-
" tioned in Virgil, the word hyda not being to
" be found in any other language but ours."

It is the opinion of the learned Dr Stukely,
" that there is no doubt our firſt Britiſh anceſtors
" were of the progeny of Abraham, in the Arabian
" line, by Hagar and by Keturah, the Iſhmaelites
" and Medianites who came hither with the Tyrian
                                    " Her-

orders of priests, who in those days kept
all their learning secret from the vulgar.
—He made every geometrical theorem a
secret, and admitted only such to the
knowledge of them, as had first undergone a five-years silence.—He is supposed
to be the inventor of the 47th proposition
of Euclid,* for which, in the joy of his
heart, it is said he sacrificed an hecatomb.
—He knew the true system of the world,
revived by Copernicus.

The

" Hercules to seek for tin."—After naming many
evidences and authorities to support this assertion,
he adds, " and these matters mutually prove one
" another, both that they came hither by sea from
" the coast of Phœnicia, and that they brought
" the arts mentioned with them from the East."

Admitting that there is merely a probability in
these opinions, it will follow, that from thence
the Druids would at once derive their theological
principles and their religious rites—the sacred
groves, the unhewn altars, the stone pillars, the
confecrated circles, emblematical of eternity, were
adopted from the manners of the Hebrews and the
eastern nations.

* The 47th proposition of Euclid, which is attributed to Pythagoras, is contained in the first
book, and is as follows.

THEOREM.

The record [appendix] alſo ſays, that
PYTHAGORAS framed a great Lodge
at Crotona, in Greecia Magna, and made
many

THEOREM,

" In any right-angled triangle, the ſquare
" which is deſcribed upon the ſide ſubtending the
" right angle, is equal to the ſquares deſcribed
" upon the ſides which contain the right angle."

The DEMONSTRATION.

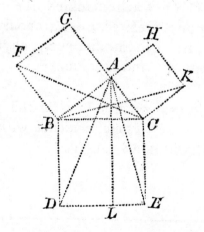

In geometrical ſolutions, and demonſtrations of
quantities, this propoſition is of excellent uſe,
and the example is held by us as a memorial of
Pythagoras.

many MASONS; fome of whom journey'd to France, and there made MA-
SONS; from whence, in procefs of
time, the art paffed into England.—From
whence it is to be underftood, that the
pupils of this philofopher, who had been
initiated by him in the Crotonian fchool
in the fciences and the ftudy of nature,
which he had acquired in his travels,
difperfed themfelves, and taught the doctrines of their preceptor.*

The fame record [appendix] fays, that
MASONS teach mankind the arts of
agriculture, architecture, aftronomy, geometry, numbers, mufic, poefy, chymiftry,
government, and religion.

I will next obferve how far this part of
of the record correfpondends with what
PYTHAGORAS taught.

The

---

* From hence it would feem that our Druids
received their origin in Gaul; but antiquaries of
late years have been of opinion that they originated in Britain.

The Pythagoric tetraƈties, were a point, a line, a furface, and a folid.—His philofophical fyftem is that, in which the SUN is fuppofed to reft in the center of our fyftem of planets, and in which the earth is carried round him annually, being the fame with the Copernican.

It feems as if this fyftem was profefled by MASONS, in contradiftinction to thofe who held the Mofaic fyftem.

Among the Jews were a fet of men who were called MASORITES: in Godwyn's Mofes and Aaron this account is given of them, " that their name was " derived from *ᗡᗡ⌐* mafar, fignify- " ing tradere, to deliver, and mafor, a " tradition, delivered from hand to hand " to pofterity without writing, as the " Pythagorians and Druids were wont " to do."

PYTHAGORAS lived at Samos, in the reign of Tarquin, the laft king of the Romans, in the year of Rome two hundred and twenty, or according to Livy,

Livy, in the reign of Servius Tullius, in the year of the world three thousand four hundred and seventy-two.—From his extraordinary desire of knowledge, he travelled, in order to enrich his mind with the learning of the several countries through which he passed.—He was the first that took the name of philosopher, that is, a lover of wisdom; which implied, that he did not ascribe the possession of WISDOM to himself, but only the desire of possessing it.*—His maxims of

---

* In Godwyn's Moses and Aaron, treating of the *Essenes*, we have the following comparisons between their principles and the maxims of *Pythagoras*.—" Their *dogmata*, their *ordinances* or con-
" *stitutions* did symbolize in many things with
" Pythagoras's: therefore my purpose is first to
" name *Pythagoras*'s, and then to proceed with
" the *Essenes*. They follow thus.

" The *Pythagorians* professed a communion of
" goods; so did the *Essenes*; they had one com-
" mon purse or stock—none richer, none poorer
" than other. Out of this common treasury,
" every one supplied his own wants without leave,
" and administred to the necessity of others: only
" they might not relieve any of their kindred
" without

of morality were admirable, for he was
for having the ſtudy of philoſophy ſolely
tend to elevate man to a reſemblance of
the

" without leave from the overſeers. They did
" not buy or ſell among themſelves, but each ſup-
" plied the other's want, by a kind commutative
" bartering: yea, liberty was granted to take one
" from another what they wanted, without ex
" change. They performed offices of ſervice mu-
" tually one to another; for maſterſhip and ſer-
" vice cannot ſtand with communion of goods.
" When they travelled, beſides weapons for de-
" fence, they took nothing with them; for in
" whatſoever city or village they came, they re-
" paired to the fraternity of the *Eſſenes*, and were
" there entertained as members of the ſame. And
" if we do attentively read Joſephus, we may ob-
" ſerve, that the *Eſſenes* of every city joined them-
" ſelves into one common fraternity or college.
" Every college had two ſorts of officers, trea-
" ſurers who looked to the common ſtock, pro-
" vided their diet, appointed each his taſk and
" other public neceſſaries; others who entertained
" their ſtrangers."

2. " The *Pythagorians* ſhunned pleaſures; ſo
" did the *Eſſenes*. To this belonged their avoid-
" ing of oil, which if any touched unawares, they
" wiped it off preſently."

3. " The

the Deity.—He believed that God is a soul diffused through all nature, and that from him human souls are derived: that they

---

3. "The *Pythagorians* garments were white; "so were the *Essenes* white also—modest, not "costly: when once they put on a suit, they "never changed it till it was worn out or torn."

4. "The *Pythagorians* forbade *oaths*; so did "the *Essenes*. They thought him a noted liar "who could not be believed without an oath."

5. "The *Pythagorians* had their elders in sin- "gular respect; so had the *Essenes*: the body or "whole company of the *Essenes* were distinguished "in four ranks or orders, according to their se- "niority; and happily if any of the superior "ranks had touched any of the inferior, he "thought himself polluted, as if he had touched "an heathen."

6. "The *Pythagorians* drank water; so did the "*Essenes* water only—wholly abstaining from "wine."

7. "The *Pythagorians* used inanimate sacri- "fices; so did the *Essenes*: they sent gifts to the "*temple*, and did not sacrifice, but preferred the "use of their holy water thereto; for which rea- "son the other Jews forbade them all access unto "the *temple*."

8. "The *Pythagorians* ascribed all things to "fate or destiny; so did the *Essenes*. In this aphorism

they are immortal, and that men need
only take pains, to purge themselves of
their vices, in order to be united to the
Deity.

" aphorifm all three jewifh fects differed each
" from other—the *Pharifees* afcribed fome things
" to fate, and other things to man's free will—
" the *Effenes* afcribed all to fate—the *Sadduces*
" wholly denied fate, and afcribed all things to
" man's free will."

9. " The *Pythagorians* the firft five years were
" not permitted to fpeak in the fchool, but were
" initiated per quinque male filentium, and not
" until then fuffered to come into the prefence
" of, or fight of Pythagoras. To this may be
" referred the *Effenes* filence at table, ftraightly
" obferved, fo that decem fimul fedentibus,
" nemo loquiter invitis novem—Drufius renders
" it, that ten of them fitting together, none of
" them fpake without leave obtained of the nine.
" When any did fpeak, it was not their cuftom
" to interrupt him with words, but by nods of
" the head or beckenings, or holding their fin-
" ger, or fhaking their heads, and other fuch-
" like dumb figns and geftures; to fignify their
" doubtings, difliking, or approving the matter
" in hand. And to the time of filence among the
" *Pythagorians*, that it muft be five years, may be
" referred the initiation of the *Effenes*; for amongft
" them none were prefently admitted into their
                              " fociety,

Deity.—He made unity the principle of all things, and believed that between God and man there are various orders of

---

"ſociety, without full trial and four years pro-
"bation.—The firſt year they received *dolobellum*,
"a ſpade; *Perezoina*, a pair of breeches uſed in
"bathing; and *veſtem albam*, a white garment
"which the ſect affected. At this time they had
"their commons allowed them, but without, not
"in the common dining hall. The ſecond year
"they admitted them to the participation of *holy*
"*matters*, and inſtructed them in the uſe of them.
"Two years after they admitted them in full
"manner, making them of their corporation,
"after they had received *an oath* truly to obſerve
"all the *rules and orders of the Eſſenes*. If any
"brake his oath, one hundred of them being aſ-
"ſembled together, expelled him; upon which
"expulſion commonly followed death within a
"ſhort time: for none having once entered this
"order, might receive alms or any meat from
"other; and themſelves would feed ſuch a one
"only with diſtaſteful herbs, which waſted his
"body, and brought it very low. Sometimes
"they would re-admit ſuch a one, being brought
"near unto death; but commonly they ſuffered
"him to die in that manner."

10. "The *Eſſenes* worſhipped towards the *Sun*
"riſing."

12. "The

of spiritual beings, who are the ministers of the supreme will.—He condemned all images of the Deity, and would have him worshipped with as few ceremonies as possible —His disciples brought all their goods into a common stock—contemned the pleasures of sense — abstained from swearing — eat nothing that had life — and believed in the doctrine of a metempsychosis or transmigration of souls.

Some eminent writers deny that Pythagoras taught that souls passed into
D   brute

---

11. " The *Essenes* bound themselves in their " oath, to preserve the name of angels:" the " phrase implying a kind of worshipping of them.

12. " They were above all others strict in the " observation of the *sabbath* day :—on it they " would dress no meat, kindle no fire, remove no " vessels out of their place, no nor ease nature; " yea, they observed every seventh week a solemn " pentecost; seven pentecosts every year.

From the great similitude in the principles of the *Pythagorians* and *Essenes*, it seems as if they were derived from one origin, varying in some few particulars suitable to the constitutions of the people : and most probably they first sprang from Egyptian tenets and maxims.

brute animals. Reuchlin, in particular, denies this doctrine, and maintains that the metempfychofis of Pythagoras implied nothing more than a fimilitude of manners and defires, formerly exifting in fome perfon deceafed, and now reviving in another alive.

PYTHAGORAS is faid to have borrowed the notion of metempfychofis from the Egyptians ; others fay from the antient Brachmans.

LEC-

LECTURE III.

On *the* Rites, Ceremonies, *and* Inftitutions *of the* Antients.

THE difciples of PYTHAGORAS were divided into two claffes; the firft were SIMPLE HEARERS, and the LAST fuch as were allowed to propofe their difficulties, and learn the reafons of all that was taught.—The figurative manner in which he gave his inftructions, was borrowed from the Hebrews, Egyptians, and other orientals.

If we examine how MORALITY or moral philofophy is defined, we fhall find that it is a conformity to thofe unalterable obligations, which refult from

D 2 the

the nature of our exiftence and the neceffary relations of life ; whether to God
as our creator, or to man as our fellow--
creature;—or it is the doctrine of virtue,
in order to attain the greateft happinefs.

PYTHAGORAS fhewed the way to
SOCRATES, though his examples were
very imperfect, as he deduced his rules
of morality from obfervations of nature;
a degree of knowledge which he had acquired in his communion with the priefts
of Egypt.—The chief aim of Pythagoras's
moral doctrine, was to purge the mind
from the impurities of the body, and
from the clouds of the imagination.—His
morality feems to have had more purity
and piety in it than the other fyftems,
but lefs exactnefs; his maxims being only
a bare explication of divine worfhip, of
natural honefty, of modefty, integrity,
public-fpiritednefs, and other common
offices of life.

SOCRATES improved the leffons
of PYTHAGORAS, and reduced his
maxims into fixed principles.

PLATO

PLATO refined the doctrine of both thefe philofophers, and carried each virtue to its utmoft height and accomplifhment; mixing his ideas of the univerfal principle of philofophy through the whole defign.

The antient mafonic record [appendix] alfo fays, that mafons know the way of gaining an underftanding of ABRAC.— On this word, all commentators (which I have yet read) on the fubject of MASONRY, have confeffed themfelves at a lofs.

ABRAC, or ABRACAR, was a name which BASILIDES, a religious of the fecond century, gave to GOD, who he faid was the author of three hundred and fixty-five.

The author of this fuperftition, is faid to have lived in the time of Adrian, and that it had its name after ABRASAN or ABRAXAS, the denomination which Bafilides gave to the Deity.—He called him the SUPREME GOD, and afcribed to

him

him feven fubordinate powers or angels,
who prefided over the heavens:—and
alfo according to the number of the days
in the year, he held that three hundred
and fixty-five virtues, powers, or intel-
ligences, exifted as the emanations of
God: the value, or numerical diftinctions, of the letters in the word, according to the antient Greek numerals, made
365 — A B P A X A Σ.
        1 3 100 1 60 1 200

Amongft antiquaries, ABRAXAS is an
antique gem or ftone, with the word
abraxas engraven on it.—There are a
great many kinds of them, of various
figures and fizes, moftly as old as the
third century.—Perfons profeffing the religious principles of Bafilides, wore this
gem with great veneration, as an amulet;
from whofe virtues, and the protection
of the Deity, to whom it was confecrated, and with whofe name it was infcribed, the wearer derived health, profperity, and fafety.

The annexed plate is from a drawing
taken in the Britifh Mufeum, of a gem
                                    de-

depofited there; is near twice the fize of
the original, which is engraved on a beril
ftone, of the form of an egg. The head
is in camio, the reverfe in taglio. The
head is fuppofed to reprefent the image
of the Creator, under the denomination
of Jupiter Ammon:*—the fun and moon
D 4   on

---

* *Jupiter Ammon*, a name given to the *fupreme
Deity*, and who was worfhipped under the fymbol
of the *Sun*.   He was painted with *horns*, becaufe
with the aftronomers the fign *Aries* in the zodiac
is the beginning of the year : when the fun enters
into the houfe of Aries, he commences his annual
courfe.   Heat, in the Hebrew tongue *Hammah*,
in the prophet Ifaiah Hammamin, is given as a
name of fuch images.   The error of depicting him
with horns, grew from the doubtful fignification
of the Hebrew word, which at once expreffes *heat*,
fplendour, or brightnefs, and alfo *horns*.

   " The *fun* was alfo worfhipped by the houfe of
" *Judah*, under the name of *Tamuz*, for Tamuz,
" faith Hierom, was *Adonis*, and *Adonis* is gene-
" rally interpreted the *fun*, from the Hebrew word
" *Adon*, fignifying dominus, the fame as *Baal* or
" *Moloch* formerly did the *lord or prince of the
" planets*.   The month which we call June, was
" by the Hebrews called Tamuz; and the en-
" trance of the fun into the fign Cancer, was in
" the Jews aftronomy termed *Tekupha Tamuz*, the
" revo-

on the reverſe, the OSIRIS AND ISIS of
the Egyptians; and were uſed hierogra-
phically to repreſent the omnipotence,
omnipreſence, and eternity of God.—
The

" revolution of Tamuz.—About the time of our
" Saviour the Jews held it unlawful to pronounce
" that eſſential name of God *Jehovah*, and inſtead
" thereof read *Adonai*, to prevent the heathen
" blaſpheming that holy name, by the adoption
" of the name of *Jove*, &c. to the idols.—Con-
" cerning *Adonis*, whom ſome antient authors
" call *Oſiris*, there are two things remarkable;
" αφανισμος, the death or loſs of Adonis, and
" ευρησις, the finding of him again : as there was
" great lamentation at his loſs, ſo was there great
" joy at his finding. By the death or loſs of
" *Adonis*, we are to underſtand the departure of
" the *ſun*; by his finding again, the return of
" that luminary. Now he ſeemeth to depart
" twice in the year; firſt when he is in the tropic
" of Cancer, in the fartheſt degree northward,
" and ſecondly when he is in the tropic of Capri-
" corn, in the furtheſt degree ſouthward. Hence
" we may note, that the Egyptians celebrated
" their *Adonia* in the month of November, when
" the fun began to be fartheſt ſouthward, and the
" houſe of *Judah* theirs in the month of June,
" when the fun was fartheſt northward; yet both
" were for the ſame reaſons. Some authors ſay,
" that

The ſtar * ſeems to be uſed as a point only, but is an emblem of PRUDENCE, the third emanation of the Baſilidian di-vine

---

" that this lamentation was performed over an
" image in the night ſeaſon ; and when they had
" ſufficiently lamented, a candle was brought into
" the room, which ceremony might *myſtically* de-
" note the return of the *ſun*, then the *prieſt* with
" a ſoft voice muttered this form of words, *Truſt*
" *ye in God, for out of pains ſalvation is come unto*
" *us.*"   Godwyn's Moſes and Aaron.

* " Our next inquiry is, what idol was meant
" by *Chiun* and *Remphau,* otherwiſe in antient co-
" pies called Repham. By Chiun we are to un-
" derſtand *Hercules,* who in the Egyptian lan-
" guage was called *Chon.* By Repham we are to
" underſtand the ſame *Hercules;* for Rephaim in
" holy tongue ſignifieth *gyant.* By Hercules we
" may underſtand the planet of the *ſun.* There
" are etymologiſts that derive *Hercules's* name
" from the Hebrew *Hiercol,* illuminavit omnia :
" the Greek etymology ἥρας κλέος, *aeris gloria,*
" holds correſpondency with the Hebrew, and
" both ſignify that univerſal light which floweth
" from the *ſun;* as water from a fountain. Por-
" phyry interpreteth *Hercules's twelve labours,* ſo
" often mentioned by the poets, to be nothing
" elſe but the *twelve ſigns of the zodiac,* through
" which the ſun paſſes yearly. But ſome may
" queſtion whether the name of *Hercules* was
" ever known to the Jews? It is probable it
                                        ' was,

vine perfon.—The fcorpion,* in hieroglyphics, reprefented malice and wicked
fubtlety, and the ferpent † an heretic;—
the

" was, for *Hercules was God of the Tyrians*, from
" whom the Jews learned much idolatry, as be-
" ing their near neighbours. It is apparent, that
" in the time of the *Maccabees* the name was com-
" monly known unto them; for *Jafon* the high
" prieft fent three hundred drachmes of filver to
" the facrifice of *Hercules*, 2 Mac. iv. 19.—The
" *ftar of Remphau* is thought to be the *ftar* which
" was painted in the forehead of *Molech*; neither
" was it unufual for the heathen to paint their
" idols with fuch fymbolica additamenta."

Godwyn's Mofes and Aaron.

The Egyptian *Apis* was to bear fuch mark.

* I own myfelf doubtful of the implication of
thefe hieroglyphics: I am inclined to believe the
whole of them implied the tenets of the Egyptian
philofophy;—that the *fcorpion* reprefents *Egypt*,
being her ruling fign in the zodiac;—and that
the *ferpent* reprefents a religious tenet. The
learned Mr. Bryant proves to us, that it was
adopted amongft the antients as the moft facred
and falutary *fymbol*, and rendered a chief object
of adoration; in fo much that the worfhip of the
ferpent prevailed fo, that many places as well as
people received their names from thence.

† —" The corruptions flowing from the *Egyp-*
" *tian philofophy*, when adapted to *chriftianity*,
" were

the implication whereof feems to be, that
herefy, the fubtleties and vices of infidels, and the devotees of fatan, were
fubdued by the knowledge of the true
God ;—the defcription I own myfelf at a
lofs how to decipher ; the characters are
imperfect, or ill copied.†

The

―――――――――――――

" were thefe : They held that the God of the Jews
" was the *Demiurgus :* that to overthrow and fub-
" vert the power and dominion of this *Demiurgus,*
" *Jefus,* one of the *celeſtial Æons,* was fent by
" the *fupreme Being* to enter into the body of the
" man *Chriſt,* in the fhape of a *dove :* that *Chriſt*
" by his miracles and fufferings, fubverted the
" kingdom of the *Demiurgus ;* but when he came
" to fuffer, the *Æon Jefus* carried along with him
" the foul of *Chriſt,* and left behind upon the
" crofs, only his body and animal fpirit : that
" the *ferpent* who deceived *Eve,* ought to be ho-
" noured, for endeavouring to refcue man from
" their flavery to the *Demiurgus.*"

Key to the New Teſtament.

† I have obtained two conſtructions of the in-
fcription on the Abrax. The one is, " The earth
" fhall praife thee, 1305," purporting the date of
the fculpture.—This date can have no relation to
the chriftian æra ; Bafilides exiſted in the earlieſt
age of chriſtianity, and the enfignæ with which the
gem is engraven, have relation, moſt evidently,
to

The MOON, with divines, is an hieroglyphic of the CHRISTIAN CHURCH, who compared I. C. to the SUN, and the CHURCH to the MOON, as receiving all its beauty and fplendour from him.

In church hiftory, ABRAX is noted as a myftical term, exprefling the fupreme God; under whom the Bafilidians fuppofed three hundred and fixty-five dependant Deities:—it was the principle of the gnoftic hierarchy; whence fprang their multitudes of thæons.—From A-BRAXAS proceeded their PRIMOGÆ-NIAL

---

to the Egyptian philofophy; which renders it probable this antique owes its creation to very remote ages. The other conftruction, without noticing the numerals, is " Terra declarat lau-" dem magnificientiamque tuam." Both thefe gentlemen fay the characters are very rude and imperfect.

As to the numerals, computing the date from the deluge, it will relate to that remarkable æra of David's conqueft of Jerufalem, and fettling the empire and royal feat there. The defcendants of Ham would probably take their date from the departure of Noah's fons from the ark.

NIAL MIND;—from the primogænial mind, the LOGOS or word;—from the logos, the PHRONÆSIS or prudence;—from phronæfis, SOPHIA and DYNA-MIS, or wifdom and ftrength;—from thefe two proceeded PRINCIPALITIES, POWERS, AND ANGELS; and from thefe other angels, of the number of three hundred and fixty-five, who were fuppofed to have the government of fo many celeftial orbs committed to their care.—The GNOSTICS * were a fect of chriftians

* " Of the gentiles who were converted to " chriftianity, the moft dangerous and pernici- " ous kind, were thofe who were infected with " the *Egyptian philofophy*; a fyftem, as it was then " taught, entirely chimerical and abfurd. The " chriftians of this fort affumed to themfelves the " name of *Gnoftics*; a word of Greek extraction, " implying in it a knowledge of things much fu- " perior to that of other men. This word doth " not occur in the New Teftament; but the *Ni-* " *colaitans* made mention of in the apocalypfe of " St. John, feem to have been of the *gnoftic fect*; " and moft of the errors maintained by *Cerinthus*, " and oppofed in the gofpel of St John, may be " derived from the fame fource. When we fay " the gentile converts were chiefly liable to the " gnoftic

christians having particular tenets of faith;
—they assumed their name to express
that new knowledge and extraordinary
light to which they made pretensions;
the word gnostic implying an enlightened
person.

The

" gnostic infection, we must not be understood
" to exclude those of the jewish race, many of
" whom were tainted with it, but they seem to
" have derived it from the *Essenes*. The main-
" tainers of the Egyptian philosophy held, that
" the *Supreme Being*, the infinitely perfect and
" happy, was not the creator of the universe, nor
" the alone independent Being: for, according to
" them, matter too was eternal. The *Supreme*
" *Being*, who resides in the immensity of space,
" which they call *Pteroma* or fullness, produced
" from himself, say they, other immortal and
" spiritual natures, stiled by them *Æons*, who
" filled the residence of the Deity with beings
" similar to themselves. Of these beings some
" were placed in the higher regions, others in
" the lower. Those in the lower regions, were
" nighest to the place of matter, which originally
" was an inert and formless mass, till one of them,
" without any commission from the Deity, and
" merely to shew his own dexterity, reduced it
" into form and order, and enlivened some parts
" of it with animal spirit. The being who at-
                                      " chieved

The gnoſtic hierarchy here pointed out, repreſents to us the degrees of etherial perſons or emanations of the Deity. —This leads me to conſider the hierarchy of the chriſtian church in its greateſt antiquity, which in the moſt remote times, as a ſociety, conſiſted of ſeveral orders of men, (viz.) RULERS, BELIEVERS, and CATECHUMENS : the rulers were biſhops, prieſts, and deacons ; the believers

were

" chieved all this they called the *Demiurgus*, the
" *operator*, *artificer*, or *workman*; but ſuch was
" the perverſeneſs of matter, that when brought
" into form, it was the ſource of all evil. The
" *Supreme Being*, therefore, never intended to
" have given it a form, but as that had been now
" done, he, in order to prevent miſchief as much
" as poſſible, added to the animal ſpirit of many
" of the enlivened parts *rational powers*. The
" parts to whom rational powers were thus given,
" were the *original parents* of the *human race*; the
" other animated parts were the *brute creation*.
" Unluckily, however, the interpoſition of the
" Supreme Being was in vain; for the *Demiurgus*
" grew ſo aſpiring, that he ſeduced men from
" their allegiance to the *Supreme Being*, and diverted all their devotion to himſelf."

Key to the New Teſtament.

were perfect chriftians, and the catechumens imperfect.

Catechumens were candidates for baptifm.—They were admitted to the ftate
of catechumen by the impofition of hands,
and the fign of the crofs.—Their introduction to baptifm was thus fingular:—
Some days before their admiffion, they
went veiled; and it was cuftomary to
touch their ears, faying, BE OPENED;
and alfo to anoint their eyes with clay:
both ceremonies being in imitation of our
Saviour's practice, and intended to fhadow out to the candidates their ignorance and blindnefs before their initiation.
They continued in the ftate of catechumen, until they proved their proficiency
in the catechiftic exercifes, when they
were advanced to the fecond ftate, as
believers.

As the DRUIDS * were a fet of religious peculiar to GAUL AND BRI-
TAIN,

---

* Tacitus faith, " among the Britains, there is
" to be feen in their ceremonies and fuperftitious
" per-

TAIN, it may not be improper to caſt our eyes on the ceremonies they uſed: their antiquity and peculiar ſtation, render it probable ſome of their rites and

E   inſti-

" perſuaſions, an apparent conformity with the " Gauls." Both nations had their *Druidæ*, as both *Cæſar* and *Tacitus* evidence; of whom *Cæſar* " thus recordeth: " The *Druidæ* are preſent at " all divine ſervice; they are the overſeers of " public and private ſacrifices, and the interpreters " of religious rites and ceremonies. They are the " preceptors of youth, who pay them the higheſt " honour and eſteem. They determine all con- " troverſies, both public and private. In the " caſes of heinous offences, murder, or man- " ſlaughter, they judge of the matter, and give " rewards, or decree penalties, and puniſhments. " They determine diſputes touching inheritance " and boundaries of lands. If either private per- " ſon or body politic obey not their decree, they " debar them from religious ceremonies, as ex- " communicate; which is eſteemed by this people " as a grievous puniſhment. Whoever are under " this interdict are eſteemed wicked and impious " perſons, and are avoided by all men, as fearing " contagion from them: they have no benefit of " the law, and are incapacitated from holding " any public office. Of the *Druidæ* there is a " chief, who hath the greateſt authority amongſt

" them:

inftitutions might be retained, in forming
the ceremonies of our fociety.—In fo modern an æra as one thoufand one hundred
and forty, they were reduced to a regular

" them: at his death the moft excellent perfon
" amongft them is elected as his fucceffor; but
" upon any conteft the voice of the *Druidæ* is re-
" quired;—fometimes the conteft is determined
" by arms.—They at a certain feafon of the year
" hold a folemn feffion within a confecrated place
" in the Marches of the Carmites (near Charhes,
" in France): hither refort, as unto the term,
" from all parts, all perfons having controverfies
" or fuits at law; and the decree and judgment
" there delivered is religioufly obeyed. Their
" learning and profeffion is thought to have been
" firft devifed in Britain, and fo from thence
" tranflated into France: and in thefe days they
" that defire more competent learning therein,
" go thither for inftruction. The *Druids* are
" free from tributes and fervice in war; and like
" thefe immunities, are they alfo exempt from all
" ftate impofitions. Many, excited by fuch re-
" wards, refort to them to be inftructed. It is
" reported, they learn by heart many verfes.
" They continue under this difcipline for certain
" years, it being unlawful to commit any of their
" doctrines to *writing*. Other matters which they
" truft to writing, is written in the Greek *alphabet*.
　　　　　　　　　　　　　　　　" This

gular body of religious, in France, and built a college in the city of Orleans.—They were heretofore one of the two
eftates

" This order they have eftablifhed, I prefume, for " two reafons ; becaufe they would not have their " doctrines divulged, nor their pupils, by trufting " to their books, neglect the exercife of the me- " mory. This one point they are principally " anxious to inculcate to their fcholars, that " man's foul is immortal, and after death that it " paffeth from one man to another. They prefume " by this doctrine men will contemn the fear of " death, and be ftedfaft in the exercife of virtue. " Moreover, concerning the ftars and their mo- " tions, the greatnefs of heaven and earth, the " nature of things, the power and might of the " Eternal Divinity, they give many precepts to " their pupils."

From Pliny we learn, " The *Druidæ* (for fo " they call their diviners, wifemen, and priefts) " efteem nothing in the world more facred than " mifleto, and the tree which produces it, if it " be an *oak*. The priefts choofe *groves of oak* " for their divine fervice : they folemnize no facri- "fice, nor celebrate any facred ceremonies with " the branches and leaves of *oak* ; from whence " they may feem to claim the name of *Dryidæ* in " Greek. Whatfoever they find growing to that
tree,

eſtates of France, to whom were committed the care of providing ſacrifices, of
preſcribing laws for worſhip, and deciding
con-

" tree, beſides its own proper produce, they eſ-
" teem it as a gift ſent from heaven, and a ſure
" ſign that the Deity whom they ſerve hath cho-
" ſen that peculiar tree. No wonder that miſleto
" is ſo revered, for it is ſcarce and difficult to be
" found; but when they do diſcover it, they ga-
" ther it very devoutly, and with many ceremo-
" nies. To that end they obſerve that the moon
" be juſt ſix days old, for on that day their months
" and new years commence, and alſo their ſeveral
" ages, which have their revolutions every thirty
" years. They call the miſleto *all-heal*, for they
" have an opinion that it is an univerſal remedy
" againſt all diſeaſes. When they are about to
" gather it, after they have duly prepared their
" ſacrifices and feſtivals under the tree, they bring
" thither two young bullocks, milk-white, whoſe
" horns are then, and not before, bound up: this
" done, the prieſt arrayed in a ſurplice or white
" veſture, climbeth the tree, and with a golden
" bill cutteth off the miſleto, which thoſe beneath
" receive in a white cloth: they then ſlay the
" beaſts for ſacrifice, pronouncing many oriſons
" and prayers, " *that it would pleaſe God to bleſs*
" *theſe his gifts, to their good on whom he had be-*
" *ſtowed them.*"

controverfies concerning rights and properties.

In the greateft antiquity in antient
Gaul and Britain, they were elected out
of the beft families, and were held both
from the honours of their birth and office
in the greateft veneration. Their ftudy
was aftrology, geometry, natural hiftory,
politics, and geography: they had the adminiftration of all facred things, were the
interpreters of religion, and the judges
of all matters indifferently.—They had a
chief or arch-druid in every country.—
They had the tutorage of youth, and
taught them many verfes, which they
caufed them to learn by heart, without
the affiftance of writing; in which manner they inftructed them in the myfteries
of their religion, the fciences, and politics.—At the conclufion of each year
they held a general feftival and affembly,
in which they paid their adoration, and
offered gifts to the GOD OF NATURE,
bringing with them mifleto and branches
of oaks; in myftic verfes fupplicating for
approaching fpring, and the renewing
year.

year.—At their facrifices,* and in their
religious offices, they wore white apparel; and the victims were two white
bulls.

---

* I cannot quit the fubject of the Druids, worfhip, without taking notice of the charge made
againft them by *Solinus* and *Dio Caffius*, " that
" they offered human victims or men's flesh in their
" facrifices."—If we examine this charge with
candour, we will not impute to them fo great an
offence againft the God of Nature and Humanity
as appears at firft fight: they were judges of all
matters civil and religious; they were the execu-
tors of the law: as being the minifters of God, to
them was committed the adminiftration of juftice.
I fhall admit that they ufed human facrifices, but
thofe facrificed were criminals; were offenders
againft fociety, obnoxious to the world for their
fins, and adjudged to be deferving of death for
their heinous wickednefs. The great attribute of
God, to which they paid the moft religious deference, was juftice:—to the God of Juftice they
offered up thofe offenders who had finned againft
his laws:—punifhments by death were of very
early date, and fuch punifhments have never been
efteemed a ftigma on the ftates in which they were
ufed.—Such executions, by the Druids, were at
once defigned as punifhments and examples: the
utmoft folemnity, and the moft hallowed rites,
preceded and prepared this tremendous exhibition,
to

bulls.—They opened a feffions once a
year, in a certain confecrated place,
in which all caufes were tried and determined.—They worfhipped one fupreme God, immenfe and infinite; but
would not confine their worfhip to
temples built with human hands; profeffing the univerfe was the temple of
the Deity; efteeming any other inconfiftent with his attributes.—Their whole
law

to imprefs on the minds of the fpectators the
deepeft religious reverence; and the utmoft horror
of the fufferings, and deteftation of the crimes
for which they fuffered, were endeavoured to be
inftilled into the hearts of thofe who were prefent
at this execution, by the doctrine of the Druids.
The criminals were fhut up in an effigy of wicker
work, of a gigantic fize, in whofe chambers of
tribulation they fuffered an ignominious death, by
burning.—This effigy reprefented the *Tyrian Hercules*, whofe name of Remphan, in the Hebrew
tongue, implies a *giant*.—With him came the
Phœnicians to this land, from whom the Amonian rites and Hebrew cuftoms were taught to the
Druids.—Under his name, worfhip was alfo paid
to the God of Nature, fymbolized by the *fun*.—
In honour and commemoration of him, the criminals were committed to his effigy, as being delivered up to the God of Juftice.

law and religion were taught in verse.—
Some Druids spent twenty years in learning to repeat those sacred and scientific
distichs, which it was forbidden to commit to writing; by which means they
were withheld from the vulgar. Such
was the aversion and enmity entertained
by the Romans against the Druids, that
(as Suetonius says) their rites were pro-
hibited by Augustus, and totally abo-
lished by Claudius Cæsar.

Many probable conjectures have been
made, that the Phœnicians * visited this
land

---

* " When we speak of the *Phœnicians*, we must
" distinguish the times with accuracy. These
" people possessed originally a large extent of
" countries, comprised under the name of the
" land of *Canaan*. They lost the greatest part of
" it, by the conquests of the Israelites under
" *Joshua*. The lands which fell in division to the
" tribe of Asher, extended to *Sydon*; that city
" notwithstanding was not subdued. If the con-
" quests of Joshua took from the *Phœnicians* a
" great part of their dominion, they were well
" paid by the consequences of that event. In ef-
" fect, the greatest part of the antient inhabitants
of

land in very early ages.—It has been attempted to be proved, from the fimilarity
of the habit worn, and ftaff carried, by
the weftern Britons.—This ftaff was ufed
by the Druids, and has the name of
Diogenes' ftaff. In a defcription given
by Mr Selden, of fome ftatues of Druids
which were dug up at Wichtelberg, in
Germany, it is particularly mentioned.—
The

" of Paleftine, feeing themfelves threatened with
" entire deftruction, had recourfe to flight to fave
" themfelves. Sidon offered them an Afylum.
" By this irruption of the Hebrew people, the
" Sidonians were enabled to fend colonies where
" ever they thought proper. *Sidon* lent them
" fhips, and made good ufe of thefe new inhabi-
" tants, to extend their trade and form fettle-
" ments. From hence that great number of co-
" lonies, which went then from *Phœnicia*, to
" fpread themfelves in all the country of *Africa*
" and *Europe*."—We may date this event about
the year of the world two thoufand five hundred
and fifty-three, and one thoufand four hundred
and fifty-one years before Chrift.
    " Spain was not the only country beyond the
" pillars of Hercules which the *Phœnicians* pene-
" trated. Being familiarized with the navigation
" of the ocean, they extended themfelves to the
                                                    " left

The Phœnicians moſt probably introduced to thoſe teachers, the laws and
cuſtoms known amongſt the antient Hebrews, and ſpecified in the Levitical inſtitutions.—The altars or temples of the
Druids, and alſo their obeliſks, or monuments of memorable events, of which
many remains are to be ſeen at this day,
bear the greateſt ſimilarity to thoſe mentioned in the Old Teſtament: Gen. xxviii.
16. " And Jacob awaked out of his ſleep,

" and

" left of the Straits of Cadiz as far as the right,
" —Stabo aſſures, that theſe people had gone
" over a part of the weſtern coaſt of *Africa* a little
" time after the war of Troy.

" We might perhaps determine their paſſage
" into England, by a reflection which the reading
" of the writers of antiquity furniſhes us with:
" they are perſuaded that all the *tin* that was
" conſumed in the known world came from the
" *iſles of Caſſitorides*; and there is no doubt that
" theſe iſles were the *Sorlingues*, and a part of
" *Cornwall*. We ſee by the books of *Moſes*, that
" in his time *tin* was known in *Paleſtine*. *Homer*
" teaches us alſo, that they made uſe of this
" metal in the *heroic ages*. It ſhould follow then,
" that the *Phœnicians* had traded in *England* in
" very remote antiquity."

De Goguet, on the Origin of Arts and Sciences.

" and faid, Surely the Lord is in this
" place, and I knew it not."—Ver. 17.
" And he was afraid, and faid, How
" dreadful is this place! this is none
" other but the houfe of God, and this is
" the gate of heaven."—Ver. 18. " And
" Jacob rofe up early in the morning,
" and took the ftone that he had put for
" his pillow, and fet it up for a pillar,
" and poured oil upon the top of it."—
Ver. 22. " And this ftone, which I have
" fet up for a pillar, fhall be God's houfe."
—Exodus xx. 25. " And if thou wilt
" make me an altar of ftone, thou fhalt
" not build it of hewn ftone; for if thou
" lift up thy tool upon it, thou haft pol-
" luted it."—Exodus xxiv. 4. " And Mo-
" fes wrote all the words of the Lord,
" and rofe up early in the morning, and
" builded an altar under the hill, and
" twelve pillars according to the twelve
" tribes of Ifrael."—Ver. 5. " And he
" fent young men of the children of If-
" rael, which offered burnt-offerings, and
" facrificed peace-offerings of oxen unto
" the Lord."—Deuteronomy xxvii. 2.
" And it fhall be on the day when ye
                                " fhall

" fhall pafs over Jordan unto the Land
" which the Lord thy God giveth thee,
" that thou fhalt fet thee up great ftones.'"
—Ver. 4. " Therefore it fhall be when ye
" be gone over Jordan, that ye fhall fet up
" thefe ftones, which I command you this
" day in Mount Ebal."—Ver. 5. " And
" there thou fhalt build an altar unto
" the Lord thy God, an altar of ftones :
" thou fhalt not lift up any iron tool upon
" them."—Ver. 6. " Thou fhalt build the
" altar of the Lord thy God of whole
" ftones, and thou fhalt offer burnt-offer-
" ings thereon unto the Lord thy God."—
It was ufual to give thofe places the name
of the houfe of the Lord. 1 Chro. xxii. 1.
" This is the houfe of the Lord God, and
" this is the altar of the burnt-offering
" for Ifrael."—This is faid of the altar
erected by David, where afterwards the
brazen altar ftood in Solomon's temple.

The oak * was held facred by the
Druids, under whofe branches they affembled

---

* *Diodorus Siculus* termeth the Gaulifh priefts
Σαρουιδας, which betokeneth the *oak*.

Bryant,

fembled and held their folemn rites.——
The oak and groves of oak were alfo
held in great veneration by the Hebrews
and other antient nations, as appears
by

Bryant, in his Analyfis, fpeaking of thofe who
held the *Amonian* rites, fays, " In refpect to the
" names which this people, in procefs of time,
" conferred either upon the deities they wor-
" fhipped, or upon the cities which they founded,
" we fhall find them either made up of the names
" of thofe perfonages, or elfe of the titles with
" which they were in procefs of time honoured."
He proceeds to clafs thofe, and reduce them to
radicals, as he terms them, and inter alias gives
the monofyllable Σαρ, *Sar*.——" Under the word
" *Sar*, fays he, we are taught, that as *oaks* were
" ftiled *Saronides*, fo likewife were the antient
" *Druids*, by whom the *oak* was held facred.——
" This is the title which was given to the *priefts of*
" *Gaul*, as we are informed by *Diodorus Siculus ;*
" and as a proof how far the *Amonian* religion
" was extended, and how little we know of drui-
" dical worfhip, either in refpect to its *effence* or
" its *origin*."
        Bryant's Analyfis of Antient Mythology."

Maximus Tyrius fays, " the Celts (or Gauls)
" worfhipped *Jupiter*, whofe fymbol or fign is the
" higheft *oak*."

The Saxons called their fages D ꝑ y̆, from the
Druids.

by Deuteronomy xii. 2, 3.—Judges vi. 19.
—1 Kings xviii. 19.—2 Kings xxi. 37.—
2 Chron. xv. 16, 17.—Deuteron. vii. 5. and
xvi. 21.—Exod. xxxiv. 13.—Judges iii. 7.*
Ifaiah i. 29. " They fhall be afhamed of
" the

---

* Deuteronomy xii. 2, 3. " Ye fhall utterly de-
" ftroy all the places wherein the nations which
" ye fhall poffefs ferved their Gods, upon the
" high mountains, and upon the hills, and under
" every green tree. And ye fhall overthrow their
" altars, and break their pillars, and burn their
" groves with fire, and ye fhall hew down the
" graven images of their gods, and deftroy the
" names of them out of that place."

Judges vi. 19. " The flefh he put in a bafket,
" and he put the broth in a pot, and he brought
" it out unto him under the oak, and prefented it."

1 Kings xviii. 19. " And the prophets of the
" groves four hundred."

2 Kings xxi. 3. " For he built up again the high
" places, which Hezekiah his father had deftroyed,
" and he reared up altars for Baal, and made a
" grove, as did Ahab King of Ifrael, and wor-
" fhipped all the hoft of heaven, and ferved them."

Ver. 7. " And he fet a graven image of the
" grove which he had made, &c.

2 Chron. xv. 16. " He removed her from being
" queen, becaufe fhe had made an idol in a grove."

Ver. 17. " But the high places were not taken
" away out of Ifrael."

Deute-

‚" the oaks which they have defired."—
The French Magi held the Δρῦσ or oak in
great veneration: *—the Celtæ revered
the oak as a type or emblem of Jupiter.†

I have been thus particular on this fubject, as it encourages a conjecture, that
the Druids gained their principles and
maxims from the Phœnicians, as appears
from thofe capital fimilarities before re-
marked: ‡ and thence it may be conceived,

Deuteronomy vii. 5. " Ye fhall all deftroy their
" altars, and break down their images, and cut
" down their groves, and burn their graven images
" with fire."
Cha. xvi. ver. 21. " Thou fhalt not plant the
" grove of any trees near unto the altar of the
" Lord thy God."
Exodus xxxiv. 13. " But ye fhall deftroy their
" altars, break their images, and cut down their
" groves."
Judges iii. 7. " And the children of Ifrael, &c.
" ferved Baalim, and the groves."

* Plin. Nat. Hift.　† Maximus Tyrius.

‡ " In the plain of Tormore, in the ifle of
" Arran, are the remains of four circles. By the
" number of the circles, and by their fequeftered
" fituation,

ceived, they also received from them the doctrines of Moses; and the original principles of wisdom and truth, as delivered down from the earliest ages.

The oak hierogliphically represents strength, virtue, and constancy, and sometimes longevity :—under these symbolic characters, it might be revered by the Druids : and the misletoe, which they held in the utmost veneration, has excellent medicinal qualities, which in those days of ignorance, might form the chief

of

" situation, this seems to have been sacred ground.
" These circles were formed for religious pur-
" poses : *Boetius* relates, that *Mainus*, son of
" *Fergus I.* a restorer and cultivator of *religion,*
" after the *Egyptian manner,* (as he calls it) insti-
" tuted several new and solemn ceremonies; and
" caused great stones to be placed in form of a
" circle : the largest was situated towards the
" south, and served as an altar for the sacrifices
" to the immortal gods. Boetius, lib. 11. pa. 15.
" Boetius is right in part of his account : the ob-
" ject of the worship was the *sun*; and what con-
" firms this, is the situation of the altar, pointed
" towards that luminary in his meridian glory.''
Pennant's Voyage to the Hebrides.

of their materia medica; being a remedy for epilepfies and all nervous diforders, to which the Britons in thofe ages might be peculiarly fubject, from the woodinefs of the country, the noxious refpiration proceeding from large forefts, the moifture of the air from extenfive uncultivated lands, and the maritime fituation of this country.

From all thefe religious inftitutions, rites, cuftoms, and ceremonies, which bear in many degrees a ftriking fimilarity to thofe of this fociety, we may naturally conjecture, that the founders of our prefent maxims, had in view the moft antient race of chriftians, as well as the firft profeffors of the worfhip of the God of Nature.   Our antient record, which I have mentioned, brings us pofitive evidence of the Pythagorian doctrine, and Bafilidian principles, making the foundation of our religious and moral rules.— The following lectures will elucidate thefe affertions, and will enable us, I hope, with no fmall degree of certainty, to prove our original principles.

F   LEC-

LECTURE IV.

The Nature *of the* Lodge.

I Now take upon me to prove my firſt propoſition, and to ſhew that the firſt ſtate of a MASON is repreſentative of the firſt ſtage of the worſhip of the true God.

The LODGE, when revealed to an entering maſon, diſcovers to him A RE-PRESENTATION OF THE WORLD;*
in

---

* " The proportion of the meaſures of the *ta-*
" *bernacle* proved it to be an imitation of the
" ſyſtem of the *world*; for that third part thereof
" which was within the four pillars to which the
" prieſts were not admitted, is as at were an hea-
" ven peculiar to *God :* but the ſpace of the twenty
                                    " cubits

in which, from the wonders of nature,
we are led to contemplate her great original, and worſhip him for his mighty
works; and we are thereby alſo moved,

F 2   to

" cubits, is as it were *ſea and land*, on which
" men live: and ſo this part is peculiar to the
" prieſts only.

" When Moſes diſtinguiſhed the tabernacle
" into three parts, and allowed two of them to
" the prieſts, as a place acceſſible and common,
" he denoted the *land and the ſea*; for theſe are
" acceſſible to all. But when he ſet apart the
" third diviſion for *God*, it was becauſe *heaven* is
" inacceſſible to men. And when he ordered
" *twelve loaves* to be ſet on the table, he denoted
" the *year*, as diſtinguiſhed into ſo many months.
" And when he made the *candleſtick* of ſeventy
" parts, he ſecretly intimated the decani, or ſe-
" venty diviſions of the planets. And as to the
" ſeven lamps upon the candleſticks, they referred
" to the courſe of the *planets*, of which that is
" the number. And for the veils, which were
" compoſed of *four things*, they declared the *four*
" *elements*. For the fine linen, was proper to
" ſignify the *earth*, becauſe the flax grows out of
" the earth. The purple ſignified the *ſea*, becauſe
" that colour is dyed by the blood of a ſea ſhell
" fiſh. The blue is fit to ſignify the *air*, and the
" ſcarlet will naturally be an indication of *fire*.

" Now

to exercife thofe moral and focial virtues, which become mankind, as the fervants of the great architect of the world; in whofe image we were formed in the beginning.

The

" Now the veftment of the high prieft being made
" of linen, fignified the *earth*; the blue denoted
" the *fky*, being like lightning in its pomegranates,
" and in the noife of the bells refembling thunder.
" And for the ephod, it fhewed that God had
" made the univerfe of *four elements*; and as for
" the gold interwoven, I fuppofe it related to the
" fplendour by which all things are enlightened.
" He alfo appointed the breaft-plate to be placed
" in the middle of the ephod, to refemble the
" *earth*; and the girdle which encompaffed the
" high prieft round, fignified the *ocean*. Each of
" the fardonyxes declares to us the *fun and the*
" *moon*; thofe I mean that were in the nature of
" buttons on the high prieft's fhoulders. And for
" the twelve ftones, whether we underftand by
" them the *months*, or whether we underftand the
" like number of the *figns of that circle* which the
" Greeks call the *zodiac*, we fhall not be miftaken
" in their meaning. And for the mitre, which
" was of a blue colour, it feems to me to mean
" *heaven*; for how otherwife could the name of
" God be infcribed upon it? That it was alfo il-
" luftrated

The CREATO'R, defigning to blefs man's eftate on earth, hath opened the hand of his divine benevolence with good gifts;—he hath fpread over the world the

---

" luftrated with a crown, and that of gold alfo,
" is becaufe of that fplendour with which God is
" pleafed."

Jofephus Antiq. Jud. cha. 7.

In another place Jofephus fays, the candleftick was emblematical of the *feven days of creation and reft:*

    " The tabernacle fet up by the Ifraelites in the
" defert, may neverthelefs give fome ideas of the
" manner in which, at that time, the *Egyptian*
" *temples* were conftructed. I believe really, that
" there muft have been fome relation between the
" tafte which reigned in thefe *edifices* and the *ta-*
" *bernacle.* The *tabernacle,* though only a vaft
" tent, had a great relation with architecture.
" We ought to look upon it as a reprefentation
" of the *temples and palaces of the Eaft.* Let us
" recollect what we have faid before of the form
" of government of the Hebrews. The Supreme
" being was equally their *God and King.* The
" tabernacle was erected with a view to anfwer
" to that double title. The Ifraelites went there
" fometimes to adore the Almighty, and fome-
                                            " times

the illumined canopy of heaven;—the covering of the tabernacle, and the veil of the temple at Jerufalem, were repre-fentations of the celeftial hemifphere, and were " of blue, of crimfon, and purple;" and fuch is the covering of the lodge.* — As an emblem of God's power, his goodnefs, omniprefence, and eternity, the lodge is adorned with the image of the

---

" times to receive the orders of their fovereign, " prefent in a fenfible manner in the prefence of " his people. I think then we ought to look upon " the tabernacle, as a work which *God* would " have, that the ftructure fhould have relation " with the edifices deftined in the Eaft, whether " for the worfhip of the *Gods*, or the habitation " of *Kings*. The whole conftruction of the taber-" nacle prefented moreover, the model of an edi-" fice, regular and diftributed with much fkill. " All the dimenfions and proportions appeared to " have beeen obferved with care, and perfectly " well adapted."

DE GOGUET.

* 2 Chron. iii. 14. " And he made the veil of " blue, and purple, and crimfon, and fine linen, " and wrought cherubims thereon."
See alfo Jofephus.

the SUN ;* which he ordained to arife from the Eaft, and open the day; thereby calling forth the people of the earth to
F 4
their

---

* Befides what is already noted touching the " *Amonian* rights and the worfhip of the *fun*, the " doctrine of the Magians was, " the *Original* " *Intelligence*, who is the firft principle of all " things, difcovers himfelf to the mind and un- " derftanding only, but he hath placed the *fun* as " his image in the vifible univerfe, and the beams " of that bright luminary are but a faint copy of " the glory that fhines in the higher heavens." It appears to the man ftudying nature, that the *fun* is the moft probable place in the univerfe for the *throne* of the *Deity*; from whence are diffufed throughout creation, light and heat : a fubtle *effence* inexhaufting, and felf-fubfifting — convey-ing, or in themfelves being, the *operative fpirits* which conduct the *works of God* through all the *field of nature*.

Pfalm civ. 1. " Blefs the Lord, O my foul. O " Lord, my God, thou art very great, thou art " cloathed with honour and majefty."

Ver. 2. " Who covereft thyfelf with light, as " with a garment."

Ver. 3. " Who maketh the clouds his chariot, " who walketh upon the wings of the wind."

Ver. 4. Who maketh his angels fpirits, and *his* " *minifters a flaming fire*."

their worſhip, and exerciſe in the walks of virtue.

The great author of all hath given the MOON to govern the night; a fit ſeaſon for ſolemn meditation.—When the labours of the day are ended, and man's mind is abſtracted from the cares of life, then it is for our ſouls recreation to walk forth, with contemplative mind, to read the great works of the Almighty in the ſtarry firmament, and in the innumerable worlds which are governed by his will; and thence to meditate on his omnipotence.*—Our thoughts returning from

---

* " O majeſtic *night !*
" Nature's great anceſtor ! day's elder born !
" And fated to ſurvive the tranſient ſun !
" By mortals, and immortals, ſeen with awe !
" A ſtarry crown thy raven brow adorns,
" An azure zone thy waiſt; clouds in heav'n's loom
" Wrought thro' varieties of ſhape and ſhade,
" In ample folds of drapery divine,
" Thy flowing mantle form, and heav'n throughout
" Voluminouſly pour thy pompous train.
" Thy gloomy grandeurs (nature's moſt auguſt
" Inſpiring aſpect) claim a grateful verſe;
" And like a ſable curtain ſtarr'd with gold,
" Drawn o'er my labours paſt ſhall cloſe the ſcene !"
                    Young's Night Thoughts.

from this glorious fcene towards ourfelves, we difcern the diminutivenefs of
man; and by a natural inference, confefs
the benevolence of that God, who re-
gardeth us (fuch minute atoms) in the
midft of his mighty works; whofe UNI-
VERSAL LOVE is thus divinely expreffed, " that not a fparrow fhall fall
" without your father; but the very hairs
" of your head are all numbered."

When the world was under the hands
of her great architect, fhe remained dark
and without form; but the divine fiat
was no fooner pronounced, than behold
there was light *——creation was delivered
from

---

* " Silence, ye troubled waves, and thou deep,
 " peace,
" Said then th' omnific word, your difcord end:
" Nor ftay'd, but on the wings of cherubim
" Uplifted. in paternal glory rode
" Far into *Chaos,* and the world unborn;
" For *Chaos* heard his voice: him all his train
" Follow'd in bright proceffion, to behold
" *Creation* and the wonders of his might.
" Then ftay'd the fervid wheels, and in his hand
" He took the golden compaffes, prepar'd
  " In

from darkneſs, and the ſun ſhot forth in-
ſtantaneous rays over the face of the
earth.—He gave that great conſtellation
to the eſpouſal of nature, and vegetation
ſprang from the embrace; the moon
yielded her influence to the waters, and
attraction begat the tides.

                              Re-

" In God's eternal ſtore, to circumſcribe
" This univerſe and all created things:
" One foot he center'd, and the other turn'd
" Round thro' the vaſt profundity obſcure,
" And ſaid, thus far extend, thus far thy bounds,
" This be thy juſt circumference, *O world.*
  " Let there be *Light*, ſaid God, and forthwith light
" Ethereal, firſt of things, quinteſſence pure
" Sprung from the deep, and from her native eaſt
" To journey thro' the aery gloom began,
" Spher'd in a radiant cloud, for yet the *Sun*
" Was not; ſhe in a cloudy tabernacle
" Sojourn'd the while.
      ——" Thus was the firſt day ev'n and morn:
" Nor paſt uncelebrated, nor unſung
" By the cæleſtial quires, when orient *Light*
" Exhaling firſt from darkneſs they beheld
" Birth-day of heaven and earth; with joy and ſhout
" The hollow univerſal orb they fill'd,
" And touch'd their golden harps, and hymning
          " prais'd
" God and his works, *Creator,* him they ſung.
                              Milton's Par. Loſt.

Remembering the wonders in the beginning, we claiming the aufpicious countenance of heaven on our virtuous deeds, affume the figures of the SUN and MOON, as emblematical of the great LIGHT OF TRUTH difcoverd to the firft men; and thereby implying, that as true mafons, we ftand redeemed from darknefs, and are become the fons of LIGHT: acknowledging in our profeffion, our adoration of him, who gave LIGHT unto his works. Let us then by our practice and conduct in life fhew, that we carry our emblems worthily; and as the children of LIGHT, that we have turned our backs on works of DARKNESS, OBSCENITY and DRUNKENNESS, HATRED and MALICE, SATAN and his DOMINIONS; preferring CHARITY, BENEVOLENCE, JUSTICE, TEMPERANCE, CHASTITY, and BROTHERLY LOVE, as the acceptable fervice on which the GREAT MASTER OF ALL, from his beatitude, looks down with approbation.

The

The fame divine hand, pouring forth
bounteous gifts, which hath bleffed us
with the fight of his glorious works in
the heavens, hath alfo fpread the earth
with a beauteous carpet: he hath wrought
it in various colours; fruits and flowers,
paftures and meads, golden furrows of
corn, and fhady dells, mountains fkirted
by nodding forefts, and valleys flowing
with milk and honey:—he hath wrought
it " as it were in mofaic work," giving
a pleafing variety to the eye of man:—
he hath poured upon us his gifts, in
abundance; not only the neceffaries of
life, but alfo " wine to gladden the heart
" of man, and oil to give him a chearful
" countenance:" and that he might ftill
add beauty to the fcene of life wherein
he hath placed us, his highly-favoured
creatures, he hath fkirted and bordered
the earth with the ocean;— for the wife
Creator having made man in his own
image, not meaning in the likenefs of his
perfon, but fpiritually, by breathing into
his noftrils the breath of life, and infpi-
ring him with that refemblance of the divinity,

vinity, AN INTELLECTUAL SPIRIT.
He skirted the land with the ocean, not
only for that salubrity which should be
derived from its agitation, but also that
to the genius of man, a communication
should be opened to all the quarters of
the earth ; and that by mutual inter-
course, men might unite in mutual good
works, and all become as members of
one society.   These subjects are represented in the flooring of the lodge.

The universe is the TEMPLE of the
Deity whom we serve:—WISDOM,
STRENGTH, and BEAUTY are about
his throne, as the pillars of his works;
for his wisdom is infinite, his strength is
in omnipotence, and beauty stands forth
through all his creation in symmetry and
order:—he hath stretched forth the heavens as a canopy, and the earth he hath
planted as his footstool:—he crowns his
temples with the stars, as with a diadem,
and in his hand he extendeth the power
and the glory:—the SUN and MOON
are messengers of his will, and all his law
is CONCORD.—The pillars supporting
the

the lodge are reprefentative of thefe divine powers.

A LODGE, where perfect mafons are affembled, reprefents thefe works of the Deity.

We place the fpiritual lodge in the vale of JEHOSOPHAT, implying thereby, that the principles of mafonry are derived from the knowledge of God, and are eftablifhed in the JUDGMENT OF THE LORD; the literal tranflation of the word JEHOSOPHAT, from the Hebrew tongue, being no other than thofe exprefs words.—The higheft hills * and loweft vallies

---

* " At length to beautify thofe holy hills, the
" places of the idolatrous worfhip, they befet them
" with trees, and hence came the confecration of
" groves and woods, from which their idols many
" times were named.—At laft fome choice and
" felect trees began to be confecrated. Thofe
" French Magi termed *Dryadæ* worfhipped the oak,
" in Greek termed Δρυς, and thence had their
" names.—The Etrurians worfhipped an holm-
" tree:—and amongft the Celtæ, a tall oak was
" the idol or image of *Jupiter*.
" Among

vallies were from the earliest times es-
teemed sacred, and it was supposed the
spirit of God was peculiarly diffusive in
those places;—Ezekiel xliii. 12. " Upon
" the top of the mountain, the whole li-
" mit thereof round about shall be most
" holy."—It is said in the Old Testament,
that the spirit of God buried Moses in a
valley in the land of Moab; implying
that from divine influence he was in-
terred in such hallowed retirement.—On
Elijah's translation, the sons of the prophets said to Elisha, " behold now there
" be with thy servants fifty strong men;
" let them go, we pray thee, and seek
" thy master, least peradventure the spirit
" of the Lord hath taken him up, and
" cast him upon some mountain, or into
" some

" Among the Israelites, the idolatry began un-
" der the Judges Othniel and Ehud, Judg. iii. 7.
" and at the last it became so common in Israel,
" that they had peculiar priests, whom they
" termed prophets of the grove, 1 Kings xviii. 19.
" and idols of the grove; that is peculiar idols,
" unto whom their groves were consecrated,
" 2 Kings xxi. 7. 2 Chron. xv. 16.
Godwyn's Moses and Aaron.

" fome valley."　Hence was derived the
" veneration paid to fuch places in the
earlieſt ages, and hence the ſacred groves
of the Eaſterns and Druids.——They chofe
thofe ſituations for their public worſhip,
conceiving that the prefence of the Deity
would hallow them : they ſet up their
altars there, and ſhadowed them with
groves, that there, as it was with Adam,
they might " hear the voice of the Lord
" God walking in the garden."

In the corruption and ignorance of
after ages, thefe hallowed places were polluted with idolatry*;——the unenlightened
mind miſtook the type for the original, and could not difcern the light from
darknefs;——the ſacred groves and hills
became

---

* " The vulgar loſing fight of the emblematical
" fignification, which was not readily underſtood,
" but by poets and philofophers, took up with the
" plain figures as real divinities. Stones erected
" as monuments of the dead, became the place
" where poſterity paid their venerations to the
" memory of the deceafed.——This increafed into
" a peculiarity, and at length became an object
" of worſhip."

Lord Kames's Sketches of Man.

became objects of enthufiaftic bigotry
and fuperftition;—the devotees bowed
down to the oaken log, and the graven
image of the fun, as being divine.—Some
preferved themfelves from the corruptions
of the times, and we find thofe fages and
felect men, to whom were committed, and
who retained, the light of underftanding
and truth, unpolluted with the fins of
the world, under the denomination of
magi among the Perfians; wifemen, fouth-
fayers, and aftrologers among the Cal-
deans; philofophers among the Greeks
and Romans; bramins among the In-
dians; druids and bards among the Britons; and with the chofen people of God
SOLOMON fhone forth in the fulnefs of
human wifdom.

The MASTER of each lodge fhould
found his government in CONCORD
AND UNIVERSAL LOVE; for as the
Great Architect moves the fyftems with
his finger, and touches the fpheres with
harmony, fo that the morning ftars together fing the fongs of gratitude, and
the floods clap their hands, amidft the
invariable beauties of ORDER; fo fhould

G   we,

we, rejoicing, be of one accord, and of one law; in unanimity, in charity, and in affection; moving by one unchanging fystem, and actuated by one principle, in rectitude of manners.

A MASON, fitting the member of a lodge, claiming thefe emblems, as the teftimonies of his order, ought at that inftant to transfer his thoughts to the auguft fcene which is there initiated; and remember that he then appears profeffing himfelf A MEMBER OF THE GREAT TEMPLE OF THE UNIVERSE, to obey the laws of the MIGHTY MAS-TER OF ALL, in whofe prefence he feeks to be approved.

The antient record which I have before quoted, expreffes that the firft mafons received their KNOWLEDGE from God; by which means they are endowed with the due underftanding of what is pleafing to him, and the only true method of pro-pagating their doctrines.

The few who remained uncorrupted with the fins of nations, and who ferved
the

the ONLY AND TRUE GOD, defpifed the fables and follies of idolaters : others who were emerging from the ignorance and blindnefs in which they had been overwhelmed, contemplated on the wonders difplayed in the face of nature, and traced the Divinity through the walks of his power, and his mighty deeds.—CONTEMPLATION at firft went forth admiring, but yet without comprehenfion from whence all things had their exiftence : Contemplation returned, glowing with conviction, that one great ORIGINAL, of infinite power, of infinite intelligence, and of benevolence without bounds, was the mafter of all.—They beheld him in his works, they read his Majefty in the heavens, and difcovered his miracles in the deep: every plant that painted the face of nature, and every thing having the breath of life, defcribed his prefence and his power.—Such men were afterwards made known to the enlightened, and were united with them in the perfection of TRUTH*.

G 2   As

---

* " Thus (as our noble author fays) through a " long maze of errors, man arrived at true reli-
" gion

As the servants of ONE GOD, our predeceffors profeffed the temple, wherein the Deity approved to be ferved, was not of the work of men's hands.—In this the Druids copied after them:—the univerfe they confeffed was filled with his prefence, and he was not hidden from the moft diftant quarters of creation: they looked upwards to the heavens as his throne, and wherefoever under the fun they worfhipped, they regarded themfelves as being in the dwelling-place of the Divinity, from whofe eye nothing was concealed.—The antients not only refrained from building temples, but held it utterly unlawful fo to do; becaufe they thought no temple fpacious enough for the SUN, the great fymbol of the Deity. " Mundus univerfus eft templum folis" was their maxim; they thought it profane

___

" gion; acknowledging but one Being fupreme
" in power, intelligence, and benevolence, who
" created all other beings, to whom all other be-
" ings are fubjected, and who directs every event
" to anfwer the beft purpofes."
                    Lord Kames's Sketches of Man.

fane to fet limits to the infinity of the Deity;—when, in later ages, they built temples, they left them open to the heavens, and unroofed.

The TRUE BELIEVERS, in order to withdraw and diftinguifh themfelves from the reft of mankind, efpecially the idolaters with whom they were furrounded, adopted emblems and myftic devices, together with certain diftinguifhing principles, whereby they fhould be known to each other, and alfo certify that they were fervants of that GOD, in whofe hands all creation exifted. By thefe means they alfo protected themfelves from perfecution, and their FAITH from the ridicule of the incredulous vulgar.—To this end, when they rehearfed the principles of their profeffion, they pronounced " that " they were worfhipers in that TEMPLE, " whofe bounds were from the diftant " quarters of the univerfe; whofe height " was no otherwife limited than by the " heavens, and whofe depth was founded " on that axis, on which the revolutions " of the ftarry zodiac were performed."

The Egyptians were the firſt people known to us, who in the early ages of the world, after the flood, advanced to any high degree of knowledge in AS-TRONOMY, ARTS, AND SCIENCES: —theſe were the means of diſcovering to them the exiſtence of the Divinity, and they worſhipped the author of thoſe ſub-lime works which they contemplated;— but through national prejudices, ſoon began to repreſent the attributes of the Deity in ſymbols; and as the viſible ope-rations of his omnipotence were chiefly expreſſed in the powers of the ſun and moon, whoſe influence they perceived through all the field of nature, they depicted the Deity by thoſe heavenly bodies, and at length, under the names of OSIRIS and ISIS, adored the GOD OF NATURE*.

As

---

* Dr Owen divides the whole of idolatrous worſhip into *Sabaiſm* and *Helleniſm;* the *former* conſiſts in the worſhip of the *Sun, Moon,* and *Stars,* and the hoſt of heaven (which only is to my pre-ſent purpoſe), which it is probable a few ages after

As we derived many of our mysteries, and moral principles, from the doctrines of PYTHAGORAS, who had acquired
G 4   his

---

after the flood had its beginning. Dr Prideaux says, " the true religion which Noah taught his poste-" rity, was that which Abraham practised, the " worshiping of one God, the supreme governor " of all things, through a *Mediator*. Men could " not determine what essence contained this power " of *mediation*, no clear revelation being then " made *of the Mediator whom God appointed*, be-" cause as yet he had not been *manifested* in the " world, they look upon them to address him by " mediators of their own chusing; and their no-" tion of the *Sun, Moon, and Stars* being, that " they were *Habitations of Intelligencies*, which " animated the orbs in the same manner as the " soul animates the body of man, and were causes " of their motion; and that these intelligencies " *were of a middle sort between God and them* " they thought these the properest things to be " *Mediators* between God and them; and there-" fore the planets being the nearest of all the hea-" venly bodies, and generally looked on to have " the greatest influence on this world, they made " choice of them in the first place, as their Gods' " mediators, who were to mediate with the Su-" preme God for them, and to procure from him " mercies and favours, which they prayed for."
He-

his learning in Egypt, and others from the Phœnicians, who had received the Egyptian theology in an early age, it is not

---

Herodotus fays that *Ofiris* and *Ifis* were two great deities of the *Egyptians*; and almoſt the whole mythology of that antient people is included in what their prieſts fabled of them. *Plutarch* conceives, that by *Ofiris* the *Sun* is to be underſtood, and this *Macrobius* confirms, adding that *Ofiris* in the Egyptian language ſignifies *many-eyed* and *Ifis* the antient, or the *Moon*. *Ofiris*, according to *Banier*, is the fame as *Mifraim*, the ſon of *Cham*, who peopled Egypt ſome time after the deluge. And *Dr Cumberland*, Biſhop of Peterborough, fays *Mifraim*, the ſon of *Cham*, grand child of *Noah*, was the firſt king of *Egypt*, and founder of their monarchy; and that *Ofiris* was an appropriated *title*, ſignifying the *prince*, and *Ifis* is *Iſhah* his wife. *Diodorus Siculus*, who has tranſmitted down to us with great care the moſt antient traditions of the *Egyptians*, aſſerts this prince is the fame with *Menes*, the firſt king of *Egypt*. Perhaps at his apotheoſis his name was changed to that of *Iſiris*, according to fome hiſtorians. As the images of *Ofiris* were very refplendent to reprefent the beams of light from the *Sun*, fo in their hymns of praife, they celebrate him as reſting in *the bofom of the Sun*.

From the authority of *Banier*, and other hiſtorians, we learn, that the gods of the *Egyptians* were

not to be wondered that we fhould adopt Egyptian fymbols, to reprefent or exprefs the attributes of the Divinity.

The

---

were adopted by the *Phœnicians*; that their *theology* was propagated *by the Phœnicians* into the *Eaft*, and in the *Weft*; and fome traces of them are found in almoft every *ifland of the Mediterranean*.

In Syria we find the fame *theology*, the *fun* under the name of *Adonis*, and the moon of *Afhtaroth*. The feftival of *Adonis* is mentioned in Baruch, chap. vii. 30, 31. " The priefts of the city fat in " their temples uncovered and fhaven, and mourn- " ing as at a feaft for the *dead*."—The prophet complains that Solomon went after *Afhtaroth*, and after Melcom, the abomination of the Ammonites.

The Chaldeans and Babylonians paid adoration to *Fire*, and held the *Sabaifm* worfhip.—The Perfians worfhipped the *Sun and Fire*.

St Cyril, writing on the *Pythagorian principles*, fays, " We fee plainly that *Pythagoras* maintained " that there was *but one God*, the original and " caufe of all things, who enlightens every thing, " animates every thing, and from whom every "thing proceeds, who has given being to all " things, and is the fource of all motion."

Pythagoras thus defines the *Divinity* :—" *God* " is neither the objeft of fenfe nor fubjeft to paf- fion;

The Pythagorian fyftem of philofophy,
alfo points out to us a reafon for the
figure of the SUN being introduced into
the lodge, as being the centre of the planetary fyftem which he taught, as well
as the emblem of the Deity which he
ferved.——This grand Μεσυρανέω was a
fymbol expreffing the firft and greateft
principle of his doctrines.——This was alfo
a re-

" fion; but invifible, purely intelligible, and fu-
" premely intelligent. In his body he is like the
" light, and in his foul he refembles Truth. He is
" the univerfal fpirit that pervades and diffufes
" itfelf over all nature. All beings receive their
" life from him. There is but one *only God*, who
" is not, as fome are apt to imagine, feated above
" the world, beyond the orb of the univerfe; but
" being all in himfelf, he fees all the beings that
" inhabit his immenfity. He is the fole principle,
" the light of heaven, the father of all; he pro-
" duces every thing, he orders and difpofes every
" thing; he is the reafon, the life, and the mo-
" tion of all beings."
Plutarch fays, " *Ofiris* is neither the *Sun*, nor
" the *Water*, nor the *Earth*, nor the *Heaven*; but
" whatever there is in nature well difpofed, well
" regulated, good and perfect, all that is *the image*
" *of Ofiris.*"
                                             Seneca

a reprefentation of the *Abrax* which governed the ftellary world and our diurnal
revolutions.

In the books of Hermes Trifmegiftus,
who was an Egyptian, and faid to be
contemporary with Abraham's grandfa-
ther, is this remarkable paffage; fpeaking of the Deity he fays, " But if thou
" wilt fee him, confider and underftand
" the fun, confider the courfe of the
" moon, confider the order of the ftars."
—" Oh

Seneca the ftoic fays, " 'Tis of very little con-
" fequence by what name you call *the firft nature*,
" and the *divine reafon* that prefides over the uni-
" verfe, and fills all the parts of it—he is ftill
" the fame *God*. He is called *Jupiter Strator*, not
" as hiftorians fay, becaufe he ftopped the flying
" armies of the Romans, but becaufe he is the
" conftant fupport of all beings.—They call him
" *Fate*, becaufe he is the firft caufe on which all
" others depend. We ftoics fometimes call him
" *Father Bacchus*, becaufe he is the univerfal life
" that animates nature;—*Hercules*, becaufe his
" power is invincible;—*Mercury*, becaufe he is
" the eternal reafon, order, and wifdom. You
" may give him as many names as you pleafe,
" provided you allow *but one fole principle*, every
" where prefent."

—" Oh thou unfpeakable, unutterable,
" to be praifed with filence."

From hence we are naturally led to
perceive the origin of the Egyptian fym-
bolization, and the reafon for their
adopting thofe objects, as expreffive of
the might, majefty, and omniprefence of
the Deity*.

Pofterity, to record the wife doctrines
and religious principles of the firft profeffors of the true worfhip, have adopted
thefe defcriptions of the lodge in which
they affemble; and maintain thofe religious

---

* The learned Dr Stukeley, fpeaking of Stone-
henge, fays he took his dimenfions of this monument by the Hebrew, Phœnician, or Egyptian
cubit, being twenty inches and three-fourths of
an inch Englifh meafure. He dates this erection
from the time of Cambyfe's invafion of Egypt, before the time of building the fecond temple at Jerufalem, at an æra when the Phœnician trade was
at its height; and he prefumes that when the
priefts fled from Egypt under the cruelties committed by that invader, they difperfed themfelves
to diftant parts of the world, and introduced their
learning, arts, and religion among the druids in
Britain.

gious tenets which nature dictates, gratitude to him under whom we exist; and
working in the acceptable service of him,
who rejoiceth in the upright man.

As such it is to be a FREE MASON;
—as such is A LODGE OF MASONS;
—as such are the principles of this society;—as these were the original institu-
tions of our BROTHERHOOD, let the
ignorant laugh on, and the wicked ones
scoff.—And that these are true solutions of our EMBLEMS, I am convinced
myself; and with humble deference to
the rest of my brethren, offer them for
their attention.

LEC-

LECTURE V.

The Furniture *of the* Lodge.

IT is with pleasure I pursue the duty I
have imposed upon myself, to give
solutions of the MYSTERIES in MA-
SONRY; which to minds inattentive to
the real import of the objects in their view,
might remain undiscovered; and the professor of masonry might pass on, without
receiving a just sense of those dignities
which he hath assumed.

I have defined what is intended to be
represented by a LODGE, and its origin
and nature; it is now my duty to discover to you the import of the FURNI-
TURE OF A LODGE.

As

As SOLOMON at JERUSALEM carried into the Jewifh temple all the veffels and inftruments requifite for the fervice of JEHOVAH, according to the law of his people; fo we MASONS, as workers in moral duties, and as fervants of the GREAT ARCHITECT of the world, have placed in our view, thofe emblems which fhould conftantly remind us of what we are, and what is required of us.

The third emanation of ABRAX, in the Gnoftic hierarchy, was PHRONÆ-SIS, the emblem of PRUDENCE, which is the firft and moft exalted object that demands our attention, in the lodge:—it is placed in the centre, ever to be prefent to the eye of the mafon, that his heart may be attentive to her dictates, and ftedfaft in her laws;—for PRUDENCE is the rule of all VIRTUES;—prudence is the path which leads to every degree of propriety;—prudence is the channel where felf-approbation flows for ever;—fhe leads us forth to worthy actions, and as a BLAZING STAR, en-
lightneth

lightneth us through the dreary and
darkfome paths of this life.

VIRTUE by moralifts is defined to be
" that ftedfaft purpofe and firm will of
" doing thofe things which nature hath
" dictated to us, as the beft and moft fa-
" lutary;—a habit of the foul by which
" mankind are inclined to do the things
" which are upright and good, and to
" avoid thofe that are evil "—In fhort,
virtue is moral honefty and good principles.

Of the VIRTUES of which PRU-
DENCE is the rule, three are called Cardinal Virtues, of which, moft properly, a
Mafon fhould be poffeffed,—FORTI-
TUDE, TEMPERANCE and JUSTICE;
for without thefe, the name of MASON is
an empty title, and but a painted bubble.

That FORTITUDE muft be the cha-
racteriftic of a mafon, I need not argue;
by which, in the midft of preffing evils,
he is enabled always to do that which
is

is agreeable to the dictates of right reafon.

TEMPERANCE alfo muft be one of
his principles, being a moderating or reftraining of our affections and paffions,
efpecially in SOBRIETY AND CHAS-
TITY.—We regard TEMPERANCE,
under the various definitions of moralifts,
as conftituting honefty, decency, and bafh-
fulnefs; and in its potential parts, infti-
tuting meeknefs, clemency, and modefty.

We profefs JUSTICE as dictating to
us to do right to all, and to yield to every
man what belongeth to him.

The CARDINAL VIRTUES, Pru-
dence, Fortitude, Temperance, and Juftice, hold in their train the inferior powers
of Peace, Concord, Quietnefs, Liberty,
Safety, Honor, Felicity, Piety, and Charity, with many others which were a-
dored by the antients in thofe ages,
when they confounded mythology with
the worfhip of the Divinity.— Within the
ftarry girdle of PRUDENCE all the virtues are enfolded.

H

We

We may apply this EMBLEM to a
ftill more religious import;—it may be
faid to reprefent the STAR which led
the wife men to BETHLEHEM, pro-
claiming to mankind the nativity of
THE SON OF GOD, and here conduct-
ing our fpiritual progrefs to the author
of REDEMPTION.

As the fteps of man are trod in the various and uncertain incidents of life; as
our days are chequered with a ftrange
contrariety of events, and our paffage
through this exiftence, though fometimes
attended with profperous circumftances,
is often befet by a multitude of evils;
hence is the LODGE furnifhed with
MOSAIC WORK, to remind us of the
precarioufnefs of our ftate on earth;—
to-day our feet tread in profperity, to-
morrow we totter on the uneven paths
of WEAKNESS, TEMPTATION, and
ADVERSITY.—Whilft this emblem is
before us, we are inftructed to boaft of
nothing;—to have compaffion and give
aid to thofe who are in adverfity;—to
walk uprightly, and with humility;—for
                                    fuch

fuch is this exiftence, that there is no
ftation in which pride can be ftably
founded:—all men in birth and in the
grave are on the level.—Whilft we tread
on this MOSAIC WORK, let our ideas
return to the original which it copies;
and let every mafon act as the dictates of
reafon prompt him, TO LIVE IN BRO-
THERLY LOVE.

As more immediate guides for a FREE
MASON, the lodge is furnifhed with unerring rules, whereby he fhall form his
conduct;—THE BOOK of his law is laid
before him, that he may not fay through
ignorance he erred;—whatever the great
ARCHITECT of the world hath dictated
to mankind, as the mode in which he
would be ferved, and the path in which
he is to tread to obtain his approbation;
—whatever precepts he hath adminiftred,
and with whatever laws he hath infpired
the fages of old, the fame are faithfully
comprized in THE BOOK OF THE
LAW of MASONRY. That book, which
is never clofed in any lodge, reveals the
duties which the great MASTER of all
exacts from us;—open to every eye,

com-

comprehenfible to every mind; then who fhall fay among us, that he knoweth not the acceptable fervice?

But as the frailty of human nature wageth war with truth, and man's infirmities ftruggle with his virtues; to aid the conduct of every mafon, the mafter holdeth the COMPASS, limiting the diftance, progrefs, and circumference of the work: he dictateth the manners, he giveth the direction of the defign, and delineateth each portion and part of the labour; affigning to each his province and his order. And fuch is his mafterfhip, that each part, when afunder, feemeth irregular and without form; yet when put together, like the building of the TEMPLE at JERUSALEM, is connected and framed in true fymmetry, beauty, and order.

The moral implication of which is, that the MASTER in his lodge fits dictating thofe falutary laws, for the regulation thereof, as his prudence directs; affigning to each brother his proper province; limiting the rafhnefs of fome, and cir-
cum-

cumfcribing the imprudence of others;
reftraining all licentioufnefs and drunken-
nefs, difcord and malice, envy and reproach : and promoting brotherly love,
morality, charity, benevolence, cordiality,
and innocent mirth; that the affembly of
the brethren may be with order, harmony, and love.

To try the works of every mafon, the
SQUARE is prefented, as the probation of
his life,—proving, whether his manners
are regular and uniform;—for mafons
fhould be of one principle and one rank,
without the diftinctions of pride and
pageantry : intimating, that from high
to low, the minds of mafons fhould be
inclined to good works, above which no
man ftands exalted by his fortune.

But fuperior to all, the LODGE is
furnifhed with three LUMINARIES*;
H 3   as

---

* The particular attention paid by the antients
to the *Element of Fire* is in no wife to be wondered at, when we confider, that when ever the
Deity deigned to reveal himfelf to the human fen-
es it was under this element.

Exodus

as the golden candleſtick in the tabernacle of Moſes was at once emblematical
of the ſpirit of God, whereby his choſen
people were enlightned, and prophetical
of the churches; or otherwiſe, as Joſephus ſays, repreſentative of the planets
and the powerful works of God: ſo our
three

Exodus iii. 2. " And the angel of the Lord ap-
" peared unto him in a flame of fire out of the
" midſt of a buſh: and he looked, and behold
" the buſh burned with fire, and the buſh was not
" conſumed."

Ver. 4. " *God* called unto him out of the midſt
" of the buſh, and ſaid, Moſes, Moſes."

Chap. xiii. 21. " And the *Lord* went before
" them by day in a pillar of a cloud, to lead them
" the way; and by night in a pillar of *fire* to give
" them light: to go by day and night."

Chap. xix. 16. " There were thunders and *light-*
" *nings,* and a thick cloud upon the mount."

Ver. 18 " And Mount Sinai was altogether on
" a ſmoke, becauſe the LORD deſcended upon it
" in *fire.*"

Chap. xviv. 17. " And the ſight of the *glory* of
" the Lord was like devouring *fire* on the top of
" the mount, in the eyes of the children of Iſrael."

Chap. xxix. 43. " And there I will meet with
" the children of Iſrael, and the tabernacle ſhall
" be ſanctified by *my glory.*"

Numb.

three LIGHTS fhew to us the three great
ftages of mafonry, the knowledge and
worfhip of the God of nature in the
purity of Eden—the fervice under the
Mofaic law, when divefted of idolatry—
and the chriftian revelation: or otherwife
our lights are typical of the holy Trinity.

H 4   As

Numb. ix. 16. " That thou goeft before them,
" by day time in a pillar of a cloud, and in a pil-
" lar *of fire* by night."

Deuteronomy v. 4. " The Lord talked with
" you face to face in the mount, out of the midft
" of *the fire.*"

Ver. 5. " For ye were afraid by reafon of the
" *fire*, and went not up into the mount."

Ver. 22. " Thefe words the Lord fpake unto
" all your affembly in the mount out of the midft
" of the *fire.*"

Ver. 23. " For the mountain did burn with *fire.*"

Ver 24. " And we have heard his voice out of
" the midft of the *fire.*"

Ver. 26. " For who is there of all flefh that
" hath heard the voice of the living *God*, fpeaking
" out of the midft of the fire (as we have) and
" lived."

To thefe may be added the fhachina in the
temple.

It would from a kind of parity in circumftances
naturally follow, that men would look up to the
Sun

Such is the furnitures of the lodge;
such are the principles dictated to us as
mafons; let us rejoice in the exercife of
thofe excellencies, which fhould fet us
above the rank of other men : and prove
that we are brought out of darknefs into
light.—And let us fhew our good works
unto the world, that thro' our LIGHT
fo fhining unto men, they may glorify
the GREAT MASTER OF THE UNI-
VERSE; and therefore " do JUSTICE
" —love MERCY—and WALK HUM-
" BLY with their GOD."

LEC.

Sun, as the *throne* of the *Divinity*, from whence
his miniftring fpirits difpenfed his will to the diftant quarters of the univerfe.—*Fire* became the
general emblem of the Divinity in the *eaftern nations*—was in great efteem with the *Chaldeans* and
Perfians. The *Perfians* ufed confecrated *fire* as
the *emblem* of the *Supreme Being*; to whom they
would not build temples, or confine the Divinity
to fpace. The *etherial fire* was preferved in the
temple of the Jews, and in the tabernacle, with
great reverence. The druid priefts in their worfhip looked towards the *Sun* :—they retained many
of the Ammonian rites:—they are faid to have
made myftical proceffions round their *confecrated
fires* funwife, before they proceeded to facrifice.

LECTURE VI.

The Apparel *and* Jewels *of* Mafons.

MASONS, as one of their firft principles, profefs INNOCENCE:—
they put on white apparel, as an emblem
of that character, which befpeaks purity
of foul, guiltleffnefs, and being harmlefs.

We have the following paffage in the
Biographia Ecclefiaftica:—" The antients
" were alfo wont to put a white garment
" on the perfon baptized, to denote his
" having put off the lufts of the flefh,
" and his being cleanfed from his former
" fins, and that he had obliged himfelf to
" maintain a life of unfpotted innocency.
" —Accordingly the baptized are both
                         " by

" by the apoftle and the Greek fathers
" frequently ftiled φωλιζομενοι, the EN-
" LIGHTNED, becaufe they profeffed
" to be the children of light, and en-
" gaged themfelves never to return again
" to the works of darknefs*.—This white
" garment ufed to be delivered to them
" with this folemn charge, ' Receive the
" white and undefiled garment, and pro-
" duce it without fpot before the tribunal
" of our Lord Jefus Chrift, that you may
" obtain eternal life. Amen.'—They were
" wont to wear thefe white garments for
" the fpace of a week after they were bap-
" tized, and then put them off and laid
" them up in the church, that they might
" be kept as a witnefs againft them, if they
" fhould violate the baptifmal covenant.

Whilft the apron with which we are
cloathed indicates a difpofition of INNO-
CENCE, and belies not the wearer's
heart, let the ignorant deride and fcoff
on:

---

* Ifaiah ix. 2. " The people that walked in
" darknefs have feen a great light: they that dwell
" in the land of the fhadow of death, upon them
" hath the light fhined."

on: fuperior to the ridicule and malice of the wicked, we will enfold ourfelves in the garb of our own virtue; and fafe in felf-approving confcience, ftand unmoved amidft the perfecutions of adverfity.

The raiment which truly implies the innocence of the heart, is a badge more honourable than ever was devifed by kings;—the Roman Eagle, with all the orders of knighthood, are inferior:—they may be proftituted by the caprice of princes; but innocence is innate, and cannot be adopted.

To be a true Mafon, is to poffefs this principle; or the apparel which he wears is an infamy to the apoftate, and only fhews him forth to fhame and contempt.

That innocence fhould be the profeffed principle of a Mafon, occafions no aftonifhment, when we confider that the difcovery of the Deity leads us to the knowledge of thofe maxims wherewith he may be well pleafed —The very idea of a GOD, is fucceeded with the belief, that

he

he can approve of nothing that is evil;
and when firſt our predeceſſors profeſſed
themſelves ſervants of the architect of
the world, as an indiſpenſible duty, they
profeſſed innocency, and put on white
raiment, as a type and characteriſtic of
their conviction, and of their being devoted to his will.—The D R U I D S were
apparelled in white, at the time of their
ſacrifices and ſolemn offices.—The Egyptian prieſts of OSIRIS wore ſnow-white
cotton.—We do not find that the prieſts
of other nations noted for antiquity were
ſingular in this, except that in the ſervice
of CERES, under whom was ſymbolized
the gift of Providence in the fruits of
the earth—the Grecian prieſts put on
white.

Every degree of ſin ſtrikes the rational
mind of man with ſome feelings of ſelf-
condemnation.—Under ſuch conviction,
who could call upon or claim the pre-
ſence of a Divinity, whoſe demonſtra-
tion is good works?—Hence are men
naturally led to conceive, that ſuch Divinity will only accept of works of righte-
ouſneſs.—Standing forth for the approbation

tion of heaven, the fervants of the firft revealed God bound themfelves to maxims of purity and virtue;—and as MA-SONS, we regard the principles of thofe who were the firft worfhippers of the true God, imitate their apparel, and affume the badge of INNOCENCE.

OUR JEWELS or ornaments imply, that we try our affections by juftice, and our actions by truth, as the fquare tries the workmankfhip of the mechanic;—that we regard our mortal ftate, whether it is dignified by titles or not, whether it be opulent or indigent, as being of one nature in the beginning, and of one rank in its clofe. In fenfations, paffions, and pleafures; in infirmities, maladies, and wants, all mankind are on a parallel;—NATURE hath given us no fuperiorities;—'tis WISDOM and VIRTUE that conftitute fuperiority.—From fuch maxims we make eftimates of our brother, when his calamities call for our council or our aid:—the works of CHARITY are from fympathetic feelings, and BENEVOLENCE acts upon the level.—The emblem of
thefe

thefe fentiments is another of the jewels
of our fociety.

To walk uprightly before heaven and
before men, neither inclining to the right
or to the left, is the duty of a Mafon,—
neither becoming an Enthufiaft or a per-
fecutor in religion, nor bending towards
innovation or infidelity.—In civil government, firm in our allegiance, yet ftedfaft
in our laws, liberties, and conftitution.—
In private life, yielding up every felfifh
propenfity, inclining neither to avarice or
injuftice, to malice or revenge, to envy
or contempt with mankind : but as the
builder raifes his column by the plane and
perpendicular, fo fhould the Mafon carry
himfelf towards the world.

To rule our affections by juftice, and
our actions by truth, is to wear a JEWEL
which would ornament the bofom of the
higheft potentate on earth;—human nature has her impulfes from defires, which
are often too inordinate:—love blinds
with prejudices, and refentment burns
with fevers;—contempt renders us incredulous, and covetoufnefs deprives us of
                                    every

4

every generous or humane feeling.—To steer the bark of life upon the seas of paffions, without quitting the courfe of rectitude, is one of the higheft excellencies to which human nature can be brought aided with all the powers of philofophy and religion.

Yet merely to act with juftice and truth, is not all that man fhould attempt; for even that excellence would be felfifhnefs:—that duty is not relative, but merely proper:—it is only touching our own character, and doing nothing for our neighbour; for juftice is an indifpenfible duty in each individual:—we were not born for ourfelves alone, only to fhape our courfe through life in the tracks of tranquillity, and folely to ftudy that which fhould afford peace to the confcience at home,—but men were made as mutual aids to each other;—no one among us, be he ever fo opulent, can fubfift without the affiftance of his fellow-creatures. Nature's wants are numerous, and our hands are filled with very little of the warfare of neceffity;—our nakednefs muft be cloathed, our hunger
satisfied.

fatisfied, our maladies vifited.—-Where
fhall the proud man toil for fuftenance, if
he ftands unaided by his neighbour?—
When we look through the varied fcene
of life, we fee our fellow-creatures at-
tacked with innumerable calamities ; and
were we without compaffion, we fhould
exift without one of the fineft feelings of
the human heart.—To love and to approve, are movements in the foul of man
which yield him pleafure : but to pity,
gives him heavenly fenfations ; and to
relieve, is divine.—CHARITY thus has
her exiftence ;—her rife is, from the con-
fcioufnefs of our fimilarity in nature ; the
level on which mortality was created in
the beginning ;—its progrefs is in fympathetic feelings, from the affections of the
heart breathing love towards our brother,
coupled with the touch of original eftima-
tion in our minds, which proves all our
fpecies to be brethren of one exiftence.--Its
conclufion is, from comparifon producing
judgment, we weigh the neceffities of
our fuffering fellow-creatures by our natural equality, by compaffion, our fympathy and our own abilities, and difpenfe
our gifts from affection.—Pity and pain
are fifters by fympathy.   To

To be an upright man, is to add ſtill greater luſtre to the Maſon's character:— to do juſtice and to have charity, are excellent ſteps in human life; but to act uprightly, gives a ſuperlative degree of excellence;—for in that ſtation we ſhall become examples in religious, in civil, and in moral conduct. It is not enough that we are neither enthuſiaſts nor perſecutors in religion, neither bending towards innovation or infidelity; not to be in the paſſive only, but we ſhould appear in the active character: we ſhould be zealous practiſers, obſervers of, and ſtedfaſt members in, religious duties.—In civil matters, we ſhould not only ſubmit to, but execute, the laws of our country; obey all their ordinances, and perform all their precepts; be faithful to the conſtitution of the realm, and loyal to our king; true ſoldiers in the defence of our liberty, and of his crown and dignity.— In morality, it requires of us, not only that we ſhould not err, by injuring, betraying, or deceiving, but that we ſhould do good in every capacity in that ſta-

tion

tion of life wherein kind Providence has placed us.

By fuch meets let the MASON be proved, and teftify that his emblematical jewels are enfigns only of the inward man : thence he will ftand approved before heaven and before men, purchafing honour to his PROFESSION, and felicity to the PROFESSOR.

LEC-

LECTURE VII.

The Temple *at* Jerusalem.

THE firft worfhipers of the God of nature, in the nations of the eaft, reprefented the Deity by the figures of the SUN AND MOON, from the influence of thofe heavenly bodies on the earth ; profeffing that the univerfe was the temple in which the Divinity was at all times and in all places prefent.

They adopted thefe with other fymbols as a cautious mode of preferving or explaining divine knowledge:—but we perceive the danger arifing from thence to religion ; for the eye of the ignorant, the bigot, and enthufiaft, caft up towards

thefe

thefe objects, without the light of underftanding, introduced the worfhip of
images, and at length the idols of OSIRIS
and ISIS became the Gods of the Egyptians, without conveying to their devotees the leaft idea of their great archetype.
Other nations (who had expreffed the attributes of the Deity by outward objects,
or who had introduced pictures into the
facred places, as ornaments, or rather to
affift the memory, claim devout attention,
and warm the affections) ran into the
fame error, and idols multiplied upon the
face of the earth.

Amongft the antients, the worfhipers
of idols, throughout the world, had at
laft entirely loft the remembrance of the
original, of whofe attributes their images
were at firft merely fymbols ; and the
fecond darknefs in religion was more
tremendous than the firft, as it was
ftrengthned by prepoffeffion, cuftom, bigotry, and fuperftition.

Mofes had acquired the knowledge of
the Egyptians, and derived the doctrines
of truth from the righteous ones of the
nations

nations of the eaſt; he being alſo touched by divine influence, and thence truly comprehending the light from out the darkneſs, taught the people of Iſrael the worſhip of the true God, without the enigmas and pollutions of the idolatrous nations which ſurrounded them.

This was the ſecond æra of the worſhip of the God of nature;—and at this period the ſecond ſtage of maſonry ariſes.

The Ruler of the Jews, perceiving how prone the minds of ignorant men were to be led aſide by ſhew and ceremony; and that the eye being caught by pomp and ſolemn rites, perverted the opinion, and led the heart aſtray; and being convinced that the magnificent feſtivals, proceſſions, ſacrifices, and ceremonials of the idolatrous nations, impreſſed the minds of mankind with a wild degree of reverence and enthuſiaſtic devotion, thought it expedient for the ſervice of the God of Iſrael, to inſtitute holy offices, though in an humbler and leſs oſtentatious mode; well judging that the ſervice and adoration of the Deity, which was only cloathed in

I 3

ſim-

I34   The TEMPLE at

fimplicity of manners and humble prayer,
muſt be eſtabliſhed in the judgment and
conviction of the heart of man ; with
which ignorance was ever waging war.

In fucceeding ages, SOLOMON built
A TEMPLE for the fervice of God, and
ordained its rights and ceremonies to be
performed with a fplendour equal to the
moſt extravagant pomp of the idolaters.

As this TEMPLE* received the fecond race of the fervants of the true God,
and as the true CRAFTSMEN were
here proved in their work, I will crave
your attention to the circumſtances which
are to be gathered from holy writ, and
from hiſtorians, touching this ſtructure,
as an illuſtration of thofe fecrets in mafonry, which may appear to my brethren

---

* Ezekiel xliv. 2. " The eaſt gate ſhall be ſhut,
" it ſhall not be opened, and no man ſhall enter in
" by it, becauſe the Lord, the God of Iſrael,
" hath entered in by it, therefore it ſhall be ſhut."
  Ver. 3. " It is for the prince: the prince ſhall
" fit in it to eat bread before the Lord."
  Ver. 4. " Then brought he me by the way of
" the north gate before the houfe."

thren dark or infignificant, unlefs they are proved from thence.

In the firft book of Kings, we are told that " HIRAM, King of Tyre, fent his " fervants unto SOLOMON: and SO-" LOMON fent to HIRAM, faying, " Behold I intend to build an houfe unto " the name of the Lord my God.—And " SOLOMON raifed a levy out of all " Ifrael, and the levy was thirty thoufand " men.—And he fent them to Lebanon, " ten thoufand a month, by courfes;— " a month they were in Lebanon, and " two months at home; and Adoniram " was over the levy.—And SOLOMON " had threefcore and ten thoufand that " bare burthens, and fourfcore thoufand " hewers in the mountains,—befides the " chief of SOLOMON's officers which " were over the work, three thoufand " and three hundred, which ruled over " the people which wrought in the work. " —And the king commanded, and they " brought great ftones, coftly ftones, and " hewed ftones, to lay the foundation of " the houfe.—And SOLOMON's builders " and HIRAM's builders did hew them,

" and

" and the ſtone-ſquarers or GIBILITES.
" —In the fourth year was the founda-
" tion of the houſe laid, and in the
" eleventh year was the houſe finiſhed
" throughout all the parts thereof, and
" according to all the faſhion of it.—
" And King SOLOMON ſent and fetched
" HIRAM out of Tyre. He was a wi-
" dow's ſon of the tribe of Napthali, and
" his father was a man of Tyre, a worker
" in braſs.—He caſt two pillars of braſs,
" with two chapiters which were of lily-
" work, and he ſet up the pillars in the
" porch of the Temple.—And he ſet up
" the right pillar, and he called the name
" thereof JACHIN; and he ſet up the left
" pillar, and called it BOAZ."—In the
ſecond book of Chronicles, we read that
" he ſet three hundred and ten thouſand
" of them to be bearers of burthens, and
" fourſcore thouſand to be hewers in the
" mountains, and three thouſand and ſix
" hundred overſeers to ſet the people a
" work.—And SOLOMON ſent to HI-
" RAM, King of Tyre, to ſend him a
" man cunning to work in gold and in
" ſilver, in braſs, in iron, in purple, in
" crimſon, and in blue, and ſkilful in
                                    " en-

" engravings.—And Hiram fent unto him
" a cunning man, endowed with the un-
" derftanding of Hiram his father.—And
" he made the veil of the temple of blue,
" purple, crimfon, and fine linen—And
" he made before the houfe two pillars,
" and called the name of that on the
" right hand JACHIN, and that on the
" left BOAZ*.

When

---

* The raifing *pillars and obelifks* was a cuftom
of the eaftern nations, and of *Egypt* in particular;
the ufe of which we are told was to *record* the
extent of dominion, and the *tributes of nations* fubject to the Egyptian empire, &c. or in *commemoration of memorable events.*—*Diodorus* tells us,
that *Sefoftris* fignalized his reign by the erection
of two obelifks, which were cut with a defign to
acquaint poftertity of the extent of his power,
and the number of nations he had conquered.
Auguftus according to the report of *Pliny*, tranfported one of thefe obelifks to Rome, and placed
it in the Campus Martius. *Pliny* fays, the
Egyptians were the firft devifers of fuch monuments, and that *Meftres* king of Heliopolis erected
the firft. *Marfham* and others attribute the invention to *Jefoftris.* The obelifk of *Shanneffes*
exceeded all that had preceded it: *Conftantine,*
and *Conftans* his fon, caufed it to be moved to
Rome, where it remains the nobleft piece of Egyptian

When this splendid structure was finish'd, " SOLOMON stood before the
" altar of the Lord, in the presence of all
" the congregation of ISRAEL, and
" spread forth his hands and said, O
" LORD GOD of Israel, there is no God
" like thee in the heaven and in the
" earth:—O LORD MY GOD hearken
" unto the cry and the prayer which thy
" servant prayeth before thee:—O LORD
" GOD turn not away the face of thine
" anointed."

In the conduct of this great work,
we must admire the sagacity of this pious
architect;—he discerned the necessity there
was to assign to portions of his people,
the

tian antiquity existing in the world. *Solomon* had
pursued this custom in erecting his pillars in the
porch of the Temple, which he designed should be
a memorial to the Jews as they entered the holy
place, to warm their minds with confidence and
faith; by this record of the promises made by the
Lord unto his father David, and which were repeated unto him in a vision, in which the voice of
God proclaimed, 1 Kings ix. 5 " I will establish
" the throne of thy kingdom upon Israel for ever."

the particular labour they were to pur-
fue; he gave them particular figns and
fecret tokens,* by which each rank
fhould be diftinguifhed, in order that the
whole might proceed with propriety, and
without confufion;—he felected thofe of
moft enlightened minds and comprehen-
five underftandings, religious men, pioufly
zealous in good works, as mafters to fu-
perintend the workmen; men fkilful in
geometry and proportions, who had been
initiated and proved in the myftical learning of the antient fages; thofe he made
overfeers of the work:—the whole was
conducted with that degree of holy reverence, that even the noife of a tool or in-
ftrument was not permitted to difturb
the facred filence on MORIALI, fanctified by the prefence of the Almighty, and
by

* Thefe were meant for the better conduct of
the work, and were totally abftracted from thofe
other principles which were the foundation of our
profeffion;—they were manual proofs of the part
each was ftationed to perform:—the light which
had poffefs'd the foul, and which was the firft
principle, was in no wife to be diftinguifhed by
fuch figns and tokens, or revealed, expreffed, or
communicated thereby.

by his miraculous works.---Was it not rea-
fonable then to conceive under this exalted
degree of pious attention, that no part of
this ftructure was to be formed, but by
men of pure hands and holy minds, who
had profeffed themfelves devoted to the
fervice of the true God, and had enrolled
themfelves under the banner of true religion and virtue.—As the fons of Aaron
alone were admitted to the holy offices,
and to the facrificial rites, fo none but
devotees were admitted to this labour.—
On this ftage, we fee thofe Religious who
had received the truth, and the light of
underftanding as poffeffed by the firft
men, embodied as artificers, and engaged in this holy work as architects.—
This together with the conftruction of the
tabernacle under Mofes, are the firft in-
ftances of our predeceffors being exhibited
to the world as builders: for altho', it is
not to be doubted, the fages amongft the
Hebrews, Egyptians, Perfians, Chaldeans,
Greeks, Romans, Bramins, Druids, and
Bards, underftood geometry and the rules
of proportion and numbers, yet we have
no evidence of their being the actual exe-
cutors of any plan in architecture.; and
yet

yet without queſtion they were the pro-
jeċtors and ſuperintendants of ſuch works
in every age and nation.

Without ſuch regulations as Solomon
had deviſed for the government of his
ſervants, without ſuch artificers, and a
ſuperior wiſdom over-ruling the whole,
we ſhould be at a loſs to account for the
beginning, carrying on, and finiſhing
that great work in the ſpace of ſeven
years and ſix months, when the two
ſucceeding temples, though much inferior, employed ſo much more time; and
when we have good authority to believe
that the temple of Diana at Epheſus, a
ſtruċture not comparable to the temple at
Jeruſalem, was two hundred and twenty
years in building.

The building being conduċted by a ſet
of Religious, makes it natural to conceive,
that from devotion and pious fervor, as
well as emulation, thoſe employed had
unceaſing motives to prompt their dili-
gence, and preſerve harmony and order;
as their labour was probationary, and led
to an advancement to ſuperior privileges
higher

higher points of knowledge, and at the laſt to that honourable pre-eminence of a MASTER of the holy work.

SOLOMON himſelf was an extraordinary perſonage, and his wiſdom and magnificence had gained him the wonder and attention of the neighbouring nations;—but this ſplendid ſtructure, the wonder of the earth, thus raiſed by the pious hands of men labouring in the worſhip and ſervice of the God of Iſrael, would of conſequence extend his fame, and attract the admiration of the more diſtant parts of the world:—his name and his artificers would become the wonder of mankind, and his works their example and emulation:—from thence the MASONS of SOLOMON would be diſperſed into different ſtates, to ſuperintend the works of other princes, and there would convert infidels, initiate brethren in their myſteries, and extend their order over the diſtant quarters of the known world.

We find that the like diſtinction was retained on rebuilding the temple in the reign of Cyrus, and that the work was
per-

performed by the religious of the Ifraelites, and not by ordinary mechanics;
for they refufed to admit the Samaritans
to a fhare of the work, although they
petitioned it, under the denomination of
fervants of the fame God:—but they
were rejected, as unworthy of the works
of piety, and unacceptable to the God of
Ifrael: for though they profeffed themfelves to be fervants of the true God,
they polluted their worfhip by idols.

JOSEPHUS, in his Hiftory of the Antiquities of the Jews, fpeaking of SOLO-
MON's going about to erect the Temple
at JERUSALEM, gives copies of the
epiftles which paffed between SOLOMON
and HIRAM of Tyre on that matter; and
which he fays remained in his days preferved in their books, and amongft the
Tyrians alfo*: which epiftles are as follow.

SOLO-

---

* Eufebius preparat. Evanget. ix. 33. 34. has
thefe letters, though greatly difguifed by Eupole-
meus, from whom Eufebius had his copies.

SOLOMON to KING HIRAM.

" Know thou, that my father would
" have built a temple to God, but was
" hindred by wars and continual expedi-
" tions; for he did not leave off to over-
" throw his enemies, till he made them
" all subject to tribute:—But I give
" thanks to God for the peace I at pre-
" sent enjoy, and on that account I am
" at leisure, and design to build an house
" to God; for God foretold to my father,
" that such an house should be built by
" me:—Wherefore I desire thee to send
" some of thy subjects with mine to
" Mount Lebanon, to cut down timber;
" for the Sidonians are more skilful than
" our people in cutting of wood;—as for
" wages for the hewers of wood, I will
" pay whatsoever price thou shall deter-
" mine."

HIRAM to KING SOLOMON,

" There is reason to bless God that he
" hath committed thy father's govern-
" ment to thee, who art a wise man, and
" endowed with all virtues:—As for my-
" self,

" felf, I rejoice at the condition thou art
" in, and will be fubfervient to thee in
" all thou requireft;—for when by my
" fervants I have cut down many and
" large trees, of Cedar and Cyprefs
" wood: I will fend them to fea, and
" will order my fubjects to make floats of
" them, and to fail to what place foever
" of thy country thou fhalt defire, and
" leave them there; after which thy fer-
" vants may carry them to Jerufalem:
" but do thou take care to procure corn
" for this timber, which we ftand in
" need of, becaufe we inhabit an ifland."

JOSEPHUS, fpeaking of the progrefs
of the building, fays, " Solomon fent for
" an artificer out of Tyre, whofe name
" was Hiram, by birth of the tribe of
" Naphthali, on the mother's fide.—This
" man was fkilful in all forts of works,
" but his chief fkill lay in working in
" gold, in filver, and brafs: the one of
" the pillars which he fet at the entrance
" of the porch at the right hand, he called
" JACHIN, and the other at the left
" hand, he called BOAZ."

SOLOMON was wife in all the learn-
K   ing

ing of the antients, he was poffeffed of all the myftical knowledge of the eaftern nations; and to perfect the fame, was enlightened by the immediate gift of hea-ven.—It was alfo the mode and manners of the times, in which the temple of Je-rufalem was erected, to ufe emblemati-cal and fymbolic ornaments in the public edifices; a fafhion derived from the hie-roglyphic monuments of the Egyptians, and the myfterious mode in which their fages concealed their wifdom and learn-ing from the vulgar eye, and communi-cated fcience to thofe of their own order only.

The pillars erected at the porch of the temple were not only ornamental, but alfo carried with them an emblematical import in their names. BOAZ being in its literal tranflation, IN THEE IS STRENGTH; and JACHIN, IT SHALL BE ESTABLISHED; which by a very natural tranfpofition may be put thus: O LORD, THOU ART MIGHTY, AND THY POWER IS ESTABLISHED FROM EVERLASTING TO EVER-LASTING:—Or otherwife they might
imply

imply, as BOAZ was the father of DA-
VID, THE HOUSE OF DAVID
SHALL BE ESTABLISHED FOR
EVER. I am juftified in this latter application, by the exprefs words of NA-
THAN the prophet unto DAVID, infpired by the vifion of the Lord,—2 Sam.
vii. 12. " And when thy days be fulfilled,
" and thou fhalt fleep with thy fathers; I
" will fet up thy feed after thee, which
" fhall proceed out of thy bowels, and I
" will eftablifh his kingdom."

Ver. 13.—" He fhall build an houfe
" for my name, and I will eftablifh the
" throne of his kingdom for ever."

Ver. 16. " And thine houfe and thy
" kingdom fhall be eftablifhed for ever
" before thee; THY THRONE SHALL
" BE ESTABLISHED FOR EVER."

In commemoration of this great PRO-
MISE to the faithful, we ornament the
entrance into our LODGES with thefe
EMBLEMATICAL PILLARS; from our
knowledge of the completion of that
facred fentence accomplifhed in the coming of our REDEEMER.

K 2   LEC-

LECTURE VIII.

On Geometry.

IT is now incumbent upon me to demonstrate to you the great signification
of the letter **G**, wherewith lodges and
the medals of masons are ornamented.

To apply its signification to the name of
GOD only, is depriving it of part of its
MASONIC import; although I have
already shewn that the symbols used in
lodges are expressive of the Divinity's being the great object of Masonry, as architect of the world.

This significant letter denotes G E O-
METRY, which to artificers, is the science

ence by which all their labours are calculated and formed; and to Masons, contains the determination, definition, and
proof of the order, beauty, and wonderful wisdom of the power of God in his
creation.

GEOMETRY is said originally to have
signified nothing more than the art of
measuring the earth, or any distances
or dimensions within it: but at present,
it denotes the science of magnitude in
general, comprehending the doctrine and
relations of whatsoever is susceptible of
augmentation or diminution. So to
geometry, may be referred the construction not only of lines, superficies, and
solids; but also of time, velocity, numbers, weight, and many other matters.

This is a science which is said to have
its rise, or at least its present rules from
the Egyptians, who, by nature, were under a necessity of using it, to remedy the
confusion which generally happened in
their lands, by the overflowing of the
Nile, which carried away yearly all

K 3   boun-

boundaries, and effaced all limits of their possessions. Thus this science which consisted only in its first steps of the means of measuring lands, that every person might have his property restored to him, was called geometry, or the art of measuring land: and it is probable, that the draughts and schemes the Egyptians were annually compelled to make, helped them to discover many excellent properties of those figures, and which speculation continually occasioned to be improved.

From Egypt GEOMETRY passed into Greece, where it continued to receive new improvements in the hands of THALES, PYTHAGORAS, ARCHIMEDES, EUCLID, and others; the elements of geometry, which were written by Euclid, testify to us the great perfection to which this science was brought by the antients, though much inferior to modern geometry. The bounds of which by the invention of fluxions, and the discovery of an infinite order of curves, are greatly enlarged.

The

The ufefulnefs of geometry extends
to almoft every art and fcience:—by the
help of it aftronomers turn their obfervations to advantage; regulate the dura-
tion of times, feafons, years, cycles, and
epochas; and meafure the diftance, mo-
tions, and magnitude of the heavenly
bodies.— It is by this fcience, that geo-
graphers determine the figure and magnitude of the whole earth, and delineate
the extent and bearings of kingdoms,
provinces, oceans, harbours, and every
place upon the globe.—It is adapted to
artificers in every branch; and from
thence, as I faid before, architects derive
their meafures, juftneffes, and proportions.

This naturally leads me to conjecture
why the SQUARE is had by mafons, as
one of the LIGHTS of MASONRY, and
part of the furniture of the LODGE.
To explain my ideas on that matter, I
will only repeat to you the words of a
celebrated author, treating of the rife
and progrefs of fciences:—He fays, " We
" find nothing in antient authors to di-
" rect

K 4

" rect us to the exact order in which the
" fundamental principles of measuring
" surfaces were discovered.   They pro-
" bably began with those surfaces which
" terminated by right lines, and amongst
" these with the most simple.—It is hard
" indeed to determine which of those
" surfaces, which are terminated by a
" small number of right lines, are the
" most simple.—If we were to judge by
" the number of sides, the triangle has
" indisputably the advantage:—yet I am
" inclined to think, that the square was
" the figure which first engaged the at-
" tention of geometricians.—It was not
" till some time after this, that they
" began to examine equilateral triangles,
" which are the most regular of all trian-
" gular figures.—It is to be presumed
" that they understood that rectilinear
" figure first, to which they afterwards
" compared the areas of other polygons,
" as they discovered them.—It was by
" that means the square became the com-
" mon measure of all surfaces ;—for of all
" ages, and amongst all nations of which
" we have any knowledge, the square
" has always been that in planimetry,
                                    " which

" which the unit is in arithmetic:—for
" though in meafuring rectilinear figures,
" we are obliged to refolve them into
" triangles, yet the areas of thefe figures
" are always given in the fquare."—
Thence I am led to determine, that the
fquare was the firft and original figure in
geometry, and as fuch was introduced to
our lodges.

The fquare was the figure under which
the Ifraelites formed their encampments
in the wildernefs, and under which they
fortified or defended the holy tabernacle,
fanctified with the immediate prefence of
the Divinity.

As I before declared it to be my opinion, that this fociety was never formed
for, or of, a fet of working architects or
mafons; but as a religious, focial, and
charitable eftablifhment, and never were
embodied, or exhibited to the world as
builders, fave only under Mofes and at
the Temple at Jerufalem, where with holy
hands they executed thofe works of piety,
as the patriarchs erected altars to the honor of the Divinity, for their facrifices and
reli-

religious offices*;—fo I am perfuaded, that the adoption of geometry by mafons, or any emblem of that fcience, implies no more than a reverence for fuch device of the mind of man as fhould demon-ftrate the wifdom of the Almighty in his works, whereby the powers of Abrax are defined, and the fyftem of the ftarry re-volutions in the heavens determined.

If we fhould look upon the earth with its produce, the ocean with its tides, the coming and paffing of day, the ftarry arch of heaven, the feafons and their changes, the life and death of man, as being merely accidents in the hand of nature; we muft fhut up all the powers of judgment, and yield our-felves to the darkeft folly and igno-rance.—The auguft fcene of the planetary fyftem, the day and night, the feafons in their fucceffions, the animal frame, the vegetation of plants, all afford us fubject

for

---

* Genefis iv. 3, 4. viii. 20. xxii. 9. xxviii. 18. xxxiii. 20. xxxi. 7.

Exodus xx. 24. xxvii. 1. xxx. 1.

Jofhua xxii. 10, 11.

for aftonifhment: the greater too mighty, but for the hand of a Deity, whofe works they are;—the leaft too miraculous, but for the wifdom of their God.

Then how much ought we to efteem that fcience, through whofe powers it is given to man to difcover the order of the heavenly bodies, their revolutions, and their ftations; thereby refolving the operations of the Deity to an unerring fyftem, proving the mightinefs of his works, and the wifdom of his decrees.

It is no wonder then that the firft inftitutors of this fociety, who had their eye on the revelation of the Deity, from the earlieft ages of the world, unto the days of its perfection under the miniftry of the Son of God, that they fhould hold that fcience hallowed amongft them, whereby fuch lights were obtained by man, in the difcovery of the great wifdom of the Creator in the beginning.

L E C-

LECTURE IX.

The Mafter Mafon's Order.

AS I at firft propofed to inveftigate the three progreffive orders of Mafons, Apprentices, Craftfmen, and Mafters, by a definition and defcription of the feveral circumftances which attended the worfhipers of the true God,—fo have I in the former lectures fhewn, that by order, in the Apprentices, is implied the firft knowledge of the God of nature, in the earlieft ages of man.—Under the Craftfmen, I have fhewn the Mofaic legation, and the Jewifh Temple at Jerufalem ; together with the light which men received, for the difcovery of the divine Wifdom, by
geo-

geometrical folutions.—I now proceed
to the third ftage, the moft facred and
folemn order of Mafons, the M A S T E R
MASON'S ORDER.

Under the Jewifh law, the fervice of
God became clouded and obfcured by
ceremonies and rites, which had daily
crept in upon it, through imitation of the
neighbouring heathen.—When the morals of the Jewifh nation were corrupted,
civil jurifdiction reeled upon its throne—
innovations fapped the religious rule, and
anarchy fucceeded.—No fooner was this
compact loofened, than the ftrength of
the Jews was diffolved, and the heathen
triumphed in Jerufalem.

The gracious Divinity, perceiving the
ruin which was overwhelming mankind,
in his benevolence, was moved to redeem
us.—He faw that the revelation which
he had deigned to make of his divinity,
might, majefty, and wifdom to the Jewifh
tribes, was not fufficient to preferve them
in their duty: he weighed the frailty of
mankind in the balance which his juftice
fuf-

fufpended, and to their deficiencies he beftowed his mercy.—The Egyptians had abufed their learning and wifdom;—the Jews had polluted God's ordinances and laws;—and Sin had made her dominion in the ftrong places of the earth.

Piety, which had planned the Temple at Jerufalem, was expunged;—the reverence and adoration due to the Divinity, was buried in the filth and rubbifh of the world;—perfecution had difperfed the few who retained their obedience, and the name of the true God was almoft totally loft and forgotten among men;—Religion fat mourning in Ifrael in fackcloth and afhes, and Morality was fcattered as it were by the four winds of the air.

In this fituation, it might well be faid, " That the guide to heaven was loft, and " the mafter of the works of righteouf- " nefs was fmitten."—The nations had given themfelves up to the groffeft idolatry; Solomon had fallen, and the fervice of the true God was effaced, from the memory

memory of thofe who had yielded themfelves to the dominion of fin.

In order that mankind might be preferved from this deplorable eftate of darknefs and deftruction, and AS THE OLD
LAW WAS DEAD AND BECOME
ROTTENESS, a new doctrine, and new
precepts were wanting to give the key
to falvation; in the language of which
we might touch the ear of an offended
Deity, and bring forth hope for eternity.
TRUE RELIGION was fled:—" Thofe
" who fought her through the wifdom
" of the antients were not able to raife
" her, fhe eluded the grafp, and their
" polluted hands were ftretched forth in
" vain for her reftoration."—Thofe who
fought her by the old law were fruftrated,
for " Death had ftepped between, and
" Corruption defiled the embrace;" Sin
had befet her fteps, and the vices of the
world had overwhelmed her.

The great Father of all, commiferating
the miferies of the world, fent his only
Son, who was INNOCENCE itfelf, to
teach

teach the doctrine of falvation;—by whom man was raifed from the death of fin, unto the life of righteoufnefs;—from the tomb of corruption unto the chambers of hope;—from the darknefs of defpair to the celeftial beams of faith;—and not only working for us this redemption, but making with us the covenant of regeneration; whence we are become the children of the Divinity, and inheritors of the realms of Heaven.

We MASONS, defcribing the deplorable eftate of religion under the Jewifh law, fpeak in figures:—" Her tomb was in " the rubbifh, and filth caft forth of the " temple, and ACACIA wove its branches " over her monument;" ἀκακία being the Greek word for innocence, or being free from fin; implying that the fins and corruptions of the old law, and devotees of the Jewifh altar, had hid religion from thofe who fought her, and fhe was only to be found where INNOCENCE furvived, and under the banner of the divine Lamb;—and as to ourfelves profeffing that we were to be diftinguifhed

by

by our ACACY, or as true ACACIANS
in our religious faith and tenets*.

   The acquisition of the doctrine of redemption, is expressed in the typical character of HURAMEN, (Ηυραμεν, inveni)
and by the applications of that name with
masons, it is implied, that we have difcovered the knowledge of God and of
his salvation, and have been redeemed
                    L   from

---

* Acacia—AKAKIA, in antiquity a roll or
bag, represented on the medals of the Greek and
Roman Emperors: some think it is only an hand-
kerchief, which they used as a signal; others take
it for a volume or roll of memorandums or petitions; and others will have it to be a purple bag
filled with earth, to remind the prince of his mortality. Acacians (Acaciani) in church history,
the name of a sect of religious and professed christians, some of whom maintained, that the Son
was only of a like, not the same, substance with
the Father; and others, that he was not only of
a distinct, but also of a dissimilar substance.—
Acacy, (in Johnson's Dictionary) ἀκακία Gr. innocence, or being free from sin.

from the death of fin, and the fepulchre
of pollution and unrighteoufnefs*.

Thus the MASTER MASON re-
prefents a man under the chriftian doctrine, faved from the grave of iniquity,
and raifed to the faith of falvation.

As the great teftimonial that we are
rifen from the ftate of corruption, we
bear the emblem of the HOLY TRINITY,
as the infignia of our vows, and of the
origin of the Mafter's order.—This emblem

---

* The mafon advancing to this ftate of mafonry, pronounces his own fentence, as confeffional
of the imperfection of the fecond ftage of his profeffion, and as probationary of the exalted degree to which he afpires, in this Greek diftich,
Τυμβοϱχοεω, Struo tumulum: " I prepare my fe-
" pulchre; I make my grave in the pollutions of
" the earth; I am under the fhadow of death."—
This diftich has been vulgarly corrupted among
us, and an expreffion takes its place fcarcely fimi-
lar in found, and entirely inconfiftent with mafonry, and unmeaning in itfelf.

blem is given by geometricians as a de-
monftration of the Trinity in Unity.

On receiving this enfign, the mafon
profeffeth himfelf in a fhort diftich, in
the Greek language, which, from the
rules of our order, I am forbid to commit to writing; the literal meaning of
which is, " VEHEMENTER CUPIO
" VITAM," ardently I wifh for life;
meaning the everlafting life of redemption and regeneration: an avowal which
carries with it the moft religious import,
and muft proceed from a pure faith.——
The ceremonies attending this ftage of

our profeffion are folemn and tremendous; during which a facred awe is diffufed over the mind, the foul is ftruck
with reverence, and all the fpiritual fa-
culties are called forth to worfhip and
adoration.

This our order is a pofitive contradiftinction to the Judaic blindnefs and infidelity, and teftifies our faith concerning
the refurrection of the body.

The divine conftruction put upon this
emblem of the Mafter's Order, which he
declares, is the principle by which he is
raifed from darknefs; fo it is alfo the
emblem of moral duties profeffed by the
mafon, and which in former ages were
moft religioufly performed. Thefe alfo
are principles immediately refulting from
the chriftian doctrine.

The MASTER MASON impofes a
duty on himfelf, full of moral virtue and
chriftian charity, by enforcing that brotherly love which every man fhould extend to his neighbour.

FIRST.

FIRST. That when the calamities of our brother call for our aid, we fhould not withdraw the hand that might fuftain him from finking ; but that we fhould render him thofe fervices, which, not in-cumb'ring or injuring our families or fortunes, charity and religion may dictate for the faving of our fellow-creature.

SECOND. From which purpofe, indolence fhould not perfuade the foot to halt, or wrath turn our fteps out of the way : but forgetting injuries and felfifh feelings, and rememb'ring that man was born for the aid of his generation, and not for his own enjoyments only, but to do that which is good; we fhould be fwift to have mercy, to fave, to ftrengthen, and execute benevolence.

THIRD. As the good things of this life are partially difpenfed, and fome are opulent whilft others are in diftrefs; fuch principles alfo enjoin a mafon, be he ever fo poor, to teftify his good-will towards his brother.—Riches alone do not allow the means of doing good; VIR-

L 3   TUE

TUE AND BENEVOLENCE are not confined to the walks of opulence:—the rich man, from his many talents, is required to make extenſive works under the principles of virtue; and yet poverty is no excuſe for an omiſſion of that exerciſe; for as the cry of innocence aſcendeth up to heaven, as the voice of babes and fucklings reach the throne of God, and as the breathings of a contrite heart are heard in the regions of dominion; ſo a maſon's prayers, devoted to the welfare of his brother, are required of him.

'FOURTH. The fourth principle is never to injure the confidence of your brother, by revealing his ſecrets; for perhaps that were to rob him of the guard which protects his property or life.—The tongue of a maſon ſhould be void of offence, and without guile;—ſpeaking truth with diſcretion, and keeping itſelf within the rule of judgment;—maintaining a heart void of uncharitableneſs, locking up ſecrets, and communing in charity and love.

FIFTH.

FIFTH. Of charity. So much is required of a mafon, in his gifts, as difcretion fhall limit;—charity begins at
home, but like a fruitful olive tree,
planted by the fide of a fountain, whofe
boughs over-fhoot the wall, fo is charity: it fpreads its arms abroad from the
ftrength and opulence of its ftation, and
lendeth its fhade for the repofe and relief of thofe who are gathered under its
branches.—Charity, when given with
imprudence, is no longer a virtue; but
when flowing from abundance, it is glorious as the beams of morning, in whofe
beauty thoufands rejoice. When dona-
tions, extorted by pity, are detrimental
to a man's family, they become facrifices
to fuperftition, and, like incenfe to idols,
are difapproved by heaven.

As Mofes was commanded to pull his
fhoes from off his feet, on Mount Horeb,
becaufe the ground whereon he trod was
fanctified by the prefence of the Divinity;
fo the mafon who would prepare himfelf
for this third ftage of mafonry, fhould
advance in the naked paths of truth,

L 4

be

be divefted of every degree of arrogance
and come as a true ACACIAN, with
fteps of innocence, humility, and virtue,
to challenge the enfigns of an order,
whofe inftitutions arife on the moft folemn and facred principles of religion.

LEC-

L E C T U R E X.

The Secrecy *of* Masons.

IN this age, when every thing serious is received with laughter, every thing religious treated with contempt, and whatever is moral, spurned from the doors of the polite; no wonder if my intentions to prove this society of religious as well as civil institution, is ridiculed and despised.

It is not to be doubted many assemblies of MASONS were held before the christian æra; the first stage of masonry took its rise in the earliest times, was originated in the mind of ADAM, descended
pure

pure through the antedeluvian ages, was afterwards taught by HAM, and from him, amidſt the corruptions of mankind, flowed unpolluted and unſtained with idolatry to theſe our times, by the channel of ſome few of the SONS OF TRUTH, who remained uncontaminated with the ſins of nations; ſaving to us pure and ſpotleſs principles, together with the original ſymbols.—Theſe antients, enlightned with original truth, were diſperſed through many ſtates;—they were called to join the Jewiſh nation; and many of them became united with that people. The WISE-HEARTED were employed in the conſtruction of the tabernacle of Moſes, they were embodied at the building of the temple at Jeruſalem, and might from thence emigrate into diſtant countries, where they would ſuperintend other religious works. The ceremonies now known to maſons, prove that the teſtimonials and inſignia of the Maſters' order, in the preſent ſtate of maſonry, were deviſed within the ages of chriſtianity, and I am confident there are not any records in being, in any nation, or in any language, which can ſhew them to be

per-

pertinent to any other fyftem, or give them greater antiquity.

In this country, under the Druids, the firft principles of our profeffion moft affuredly were taught and exercifed: how foon the fecond ftage and its ceremonials were promulged after the building of the temple at Jerufalem, we have no degree of evidence. As to the third and moft facred order, no doubt it was adopted upon the converfion of thofe who attended the DRUIDICAL WORSHIP, who had profeffed the adoration of the ONE SUPREME BEING, and who readily would receive the doctrines of a MEDIATOR; a fyftem in religion which had led the fages of old into innumerable errors, and at laft confounded them with idolatry.

Under our prefent profeffion of mafonry, we alledge our morality was originally deduced from the fchool of Pythagoras, and that the Bafilidian fyftem of religion furnifhed us with fome tenets, principles, and hieroglyphics: but thefe, together with the Egyptian fymbols and Judaic monuments, are collected only as a fuca successional series of circumstances, which the devotees of the Deity, in different and distant ages of the world, had professed; and are all resolved into the present system of masonry, which is made perfect in the doctrine of christianity: from these united members gaining alone that evidence of antiquity, which shews that we are descendants of the first worshippers of the Deity.

That there were builders of cities, towers, temples, and fortifications, from the earliest ages, is indisputable;—but that the artificers were formed into bodies, ruled by their own proper laws, and knowing mysteries and secrets which were kept from the world, I am greatly doubtful:—for so plain, easy, and intelligible is the mechanic art of building, that it is comprehensible to any capacity, and needed not to be wrapped up in mystic rules; neither was there any occasion for the artificers to go about as conjurers, professing a science unrevealed to the world.

Man

Man would be taught building by the
animals daily under his obfervation: the
fox, the rabbit, and many other creatures, form themfelves caves; the beaver
is an architect in wood, and builds hovels
and fheds; the birds at a feafon for their
increafe, prepare their nefts for the protection of their young; the bee labours in
conftructing cities and ftore-houfes; the
ants are cloiftered in their little mount,
perforated with labyrinths, where their
provender and progeny are fecured.—All
thefe would inftruct men in building;—
fo that whilft our race were reaping the
firft rudiments of knowledge from the
book of nature, after the darknefs which
had overwhelmed them in their difobe-
dience, this could remain no fecret.

Befides, if we fhould be refolved into
the fucceffors of mechanics, and as fuch,
fhould take our grand progrefs from the
building of the temple at Jerufalem, we
fhall find, that HIRAM, who was fent
from Tyre to affift in that ftructure, had
not his excellence in architecture only,
but in molten work, and alfo in dying,

as

as is faid in Chronicles : " He was fkilful
" to work in filver and gold, in brafs, in
" iron, in ftone, and in timber, in pur-
" ple, in blue, in fine linen, and in crim-
" fon; alfo to grave all manner of gra-
" ving."—He was the fubject of a ftate,
wherein the worfhip of idols was eftablifhed.—This kind of religion gave encouragement to, and greatly advanced
the fine arts, as it employed ftatuaries,
fculptors, painters, and thofe who made
graven images.—Solomon ornamented his
temple with cherubins and palm trees,
fruits and flowers : from whence I do not
doubt Hiram's knowledge was in the bu-
finefs of a ftatuary and painter, that he
made graven images of ftone and wood,
and molten images in metals.—In Kings,
it is faid only, " that Hiram was filled
" with wifdom and underftanding, and
cunning to work all works in brafs."—
As to Solomon's part in this great ftructure, he being inclined to this mighty
work of piety through the ordinances of
heaven, and the promifes made to his father David, was the executor of that
plan which was revealed to him from a-
bove :—he called forth the fages and religious

gious men amongſt his people to perform
the work:—he claſſed them according to
their rank in their religious profeſſion; as
the prieſts of the temple were ſtationed in
the ſolemn rites and ceremonies inſtituted
there.—This diſtinction was maintained
in moſt religious ſocieties, but eſpecially
with the primitive chriſtians.—The choſen ones of Solomon, as a pious and holy
duty, conducted the work.—If we regard
them as architects by profeſſion, by reaſon
of this duty, ſo we may Abel, Noah,
Abraham, Jacob, Moſes, and David, by
reaſon of the building of their altars,
which were no other than works of piety
and devotion.—From thoſe circumſtances,
I am bold to ſay, that if we trace the
antiquity of maſonry on the operative
principles, and derive ſuch principles from
the building of Solomon's Temple, we
may as well claim all the profeſſions which
Hiram excelled in:—but I will leave this
ſpeculation for more material ſubjects.

Some maſters of deſign have brought
their works to a ſingular juſtneſs, ſym-
metry, and order, in Egypt and Greece,
in Italy and many other European ſtates:
but

but they, like proficients in painting and mufic, had their excellence from a degree of genius and tafte peculiar to themfelves. —It was a fingular gift, and they needed not myfteries to keep it fecret; for as men's geniufes are as various as their features, fo was this excellence in architecture as free from ufurpation, as if it had been wrapped up in the moft profound magic.

I am perfuaded there was no occafion to form fuch fecret rules for the compact of operative mafons:—Solomon, for the conduct of fuch a multitude, wifely preferved the order of the religious, and the myfteries of their initiation, for the rule of his people employed in the temple.—Affuredly the fecrets revealed to us were for other ufes than what relate to labouring up maffes of ftone; and our fociety, as it now ftands, is an affociation on religious and charitable principles; which principles were inftituted and arofe upon the knowledge of God, and in the chriftian revelation

Soon

Soon after the time that christianity became the established religion of this country, the professors of it employed themselves in founding religious houses, and in the building of places of public worship.—On any reform of religion, it is observable the first professors are inclinable to enthusiasm.—Such was the case in this land, on the advancement of the christian doctrine:—a fervor for endowments infatuated the minds of the converted;—certain days were assigned for the purpose of attending to religious works and edifices, called hally-warkdays; on which no man, of what profession, rank, or estate soever, was exempt from attending that duty.—Besides, there were a set of men called haly-werkfolk*, to whom were assigned certain

M   lands,

---

* De Hermitorio Finchalensis Ranulphus Dei gratia Dunelmensis Episcopus omnibus hominibus suis Francis et Anglis de haly werc folc salutem, &c.

Many other grants are in my possession of this kind. Ralph Flamberd was confecrated Bishop of Durham in 1099.

lands, which they held by the fervice of repairing, defending, or building churches and fepulchres ; for which pious labours they were exempt from all feodal and military fervices : thefe men being ftone-cutters and builders, might alfo be of our profeffion, and moft probably they were felected from thence, the two being in no wife incompatible with each other.—The county of Durham * entertained a particular fet of thofe haly-werk-folk, who were guards of the patrimony and holy fepulchre of St Cuthbert.—Thefe men come the neareft to a fimilitude of Solomon's mafons, and to the title of FREE AND ACCEPTED MASONS, of any degree of architects I have gained any knowledge of : but whether their initiation was attended with any peculiar ceremonies, or by what laws they were regulated, I have not been able to difcover ; and muft lament, that in the church records of Durham, or in any public office there, there are not the leaft remains of evidence, touching thefe people and the con-

* Hift. Dunelm. apud Wartoni Aug. Sax.

ſtitution of their ſociety. It was a matter
to be coveted by me, lecturing on this
ſubject, as moſt probably ſuch conſtitution
or evidence would have confirmed every
hypotheſis I have raiſed on the definition
of our emblems and myſteries.

The emblems uſed by theſe people,
very much reſembled thoſe of our ſociety,
ſeveral tokens of which have been found
of late years in pulling down old ruins.—
It is much to be wiſhed, that thoſe noble-
men, &c. in whoſe poſſeſſion antient abbeys ſtand, would on all occaſions of pulling down or repairing, give inſtructions
to their workmen, to preſerve with care
any antique marks, characters, or emblems they may find.—There are ſome
double walls, or hollow pillars, in which
ſuch things were depoſited. — Few men
will be at the expence of digging to the
foundations of ſuch buildings, where
valuable marks and curious inſcriptions
would be found on the foundation or
what was called the angle-ſtone, which
formed a perfect cube.—This was a very
antient cuſtom: the unbelieving Jews ac-
cuſed our Saviour of having ſtolen the

myſtic

myftic words, the TETRAGRAMMA-
TON, or URIM AND THUMMIM,
from the foundation of the temple at
Jerufalem, which they faid he carried
concealed about him, whereby he was
enabled to work his miracles.

Soon after the progrefs of chriftianity
in this land, all Europe was inflamed with
the cry and madnefs of an enthufiaftic
monk, who prompted the zealots in religion to the holy war; in which, for the
purpofe of recovering the holy city and
Judea out of the hands of infidels, armed
legions of faints, devotees, and enthu-
fiafts, in tens of thoufands, poured forth
from every ftate of Europe, to wafte their
blood and treafure, in a purpofe as barren
and unprofitable as impolitic.

It was deemed neceffary that thofe
who took up the enfign of the crofs in
this enterprize, fhould form themfelves
into fuch focieties as might fecure them
from fpies and treacheries; and that
each might know his companion and
brother labourer, as well in the dark as
by day. As it was with Jeptha's army
at

at the paffes of Jordan, fo alfo was
it requifite in thefe expeditions that
certain figns, fignals, watch-words, or
pafs-words, fhould be known amongft
them; for the armies confifted of various
nations and various languages.—We are
told in the book of Judges, " that the
" Gileadites took the paffes of Jordan
" before the Ephraimites; and it was fo,
" that when thofe Ephraimites which
" were efcaped faid, let me go over, that
" the men of Gilead faid unto him, Art
" thou an Ephraimite? If he faid nay,
" then faid they unto him, fay now Shib-
" boleth, and he faid Sibboleth, for he
" could not frame to pronounce it right.
" Then they took them and flew them at
" the paffage of Jordan.*"

M 3　　　　　　　No

* The application which is made of the word *Sibboleth* amongft mafons, is as a teftimony of their retaining their *original vow* uninfringed, and their firft
faith with the brotherhood uncorrupted. And to
render their words and phrafes more abftrufe and
obfcure, they felected fuch as by acceptation in the
fcriptures, or otherwife, might puzzle the ignorant
by a double implication.—Thus *Sibboleth,* fhould we
have

No project or device could answer the
purposes of the crusadors better than those
of masonry:--the maxims and ceremonials
attending the Master's order had been
pre-

---

have adopted the Elusimian mysteries, would answer as an avowal of our profession, the same implying, *Ears of Corn*; but it has its etymology
or derivation from the following compounds in
the Greek tongue, as it is adopted by masons,
viz. Σιβο, Colo, and Λιθος, Lapis; so Σιβο-λιθον,
Sibbolithon, *Colo Lapidem*, implies, that they retain and keep inviolate their obligations, as the
Juramentum per Jovem Lapidem, the most obligatory oath held amongst the heathen.—" The name
" Lapis, or, as others write, Lapideus, was given
" to Jupiter by the Romans, who conceived that
" Juramentum per Jovem Lapidem, an oath by
" Jupiter Lapis, was the most obligatory oath;
" and it is derived either from the stone which was
" presented to Saturn by his wife Ops, who said
" that it was Jupiter, in which sense Eusebius
" says that Lapis reigned in Crete: or from lipide
" silice, the flint stone, which in making bargains
" the swearer held in his hand and said, ' If
" knowingly I deceive, so let Diespiter, saving
" the city and the capital, cast me away from all
" that's good, as I cast away this stone.' Where-
" upon he threw the stone away."

                                           Pantheon.

previously eftablifhed, and were materi-
ally neceffary on that expedition ; for as
the Mahomedans were alfo worfhippers of
the Deity, and as the enterprizers were
feeking a country where the mafons were
in the time of Solomon called into an
affociation, and where fome remains would
certainly be found of the myfteries and
wifdom of the antients and of our predeceffors. Such degrees of mafonry as extended only to the acknowledgment of
their being fervants of the God of nature,
would not have diftinguifhed them from
thofe they had to encounter, had they
not affumed the fymbols of the chriftian
faith.

All the learning of Europe in thofe
times, as in the ages of antiquity, was
poffeffed by the religious ;—they had acquired the wifdom of the antients, and
the original knowledge which was in the
beginning, and now is, THE TRUTH;
—many of them had been initiated into
the myfteries of mafonry ;—they were the
projectors of this enterprize, and as Solomon in the building of the temple, introduced orders and regulations for the con-

duct

duct of the work, which his wifdom had
been enriched with from the learning of
the fages of antiquity, fo that no confufion fhould happen during its progrefs,
and fo that the rank and office of each
fellow-labourer might be diftinguifhed and
afcertained beyond the poffibility of de-
ceit; in like manner the priefts projecting
the crufades, being poffeffed of the myfteries of mafonry, the knowledge of the
antients, and of the univerfal language
which furvived the confufion of Shinar,
revived the orders and regulations of Solomon, and initiated the legions therein
who followed them to the Holy Land:—
hence that fecrecy which attended the
crufaders.

Amongft other evidence which autho-
rizes me in the conjecture that mafons
went to the holy wars, is the doctrine of
that order of mafons, called the HIGHER
ORDER. I am induced to believe that
order was of Scottifh extraction; feparate
nations might be diftinguifhed by fome
feparate order, as they were by fingular
enfigns : but be that as it may, it fully
proves to me that mafons were crufaders.

As

As my intention in this lecture was not only to fpeculate on the antient fe-crecy amongft mafons, but alfo to treat of the fecrecy of mafons in this age, I muft therefore turn my thoughts to the importance fecrefy is now of amongft us; when there are no holy ftructures to erect, no holy wars to wage, and nothing but charity and brotherly love to cherifh a-mong mafons.

This inftitution, which was firft founded in the myfteries of religion, as I have be-fore rehearfed to you, is now maintained by us on the principles of lending mutual aid and confolation to each other.—How fhould we be able to difcern the brethren of this family, but through fuch tokens as fhould point them out from other men? Language is now provincial, and the dia-lects of different nations would not be comprehenfible to men ignorant and un-lettered. Hence it became neceffary to ufe an expreffion which fhould be cog-nizable by people of all nations.—So it is with mafons;—they are poffeffed of that univerfal expreffion, and of fuch remains

of

of the original language, that they can communicate their hiftory, their wants, and prayers, to every brother mafon throughout the globe:—from whence, it is certain, that multitudes of lives have been faved in foreign countries, when fhip-wreck and mifery had overwhelmed them: when robbers had pillaged, when ficknefs, want, and mifery had brought them even to the brink of the grave, the difcovery of mafonry has faved them: the difcovery of being a brother, hath ftaid the favage hand of the conqueror, lifted in the field of battle to cut off the captive; hath withheld the fword im-brued in carnage and flaughter, and fub-dued the infolence of triumph to pay homage to the craft.

The importance of fecrecy with us, is fuch, that we may not be deceived in the difpenfing of our charities;—that we may not be betrayed in the tendernefs of our benevolence, and others ufurp the portion which is prepared for thofe of our own family.

Te

To betray the watch-word, which
fhould keep the enemy from the walls
of our citadel, fo as to open our ftrong-
holds to robbers and deceivers, is as great
a moral crime, as to fhew the common
thief the weakneffes and fecret places of
our neighbour's dwelling-houfes, that he
may pillage their goods.—Nay it is ftill
greater, for it is like aiding the facrile-
gious robber to ranfack the holy places,
and fteal the facred veffels devoted to
the moft folemn rites of religion.—It is
fnatching from the divine hand of charity, the balm which fhe holds forth to
heal the diftreffes of her children; the cor-
dial cup of confolation, which fhe offers
to the lip of calamity, and the fuftenance
her fainting infants fhould receive from
the bofom of her celeftial love.

As this then is the importance of mafons fecrecy, wherefore fhould the world
wonder that the moft profligate tongue
which ever had expreffion hath not revealed it? The fport is too criminal to
afford delight even to the wickedeft of
mankind; for it muft be wantonnefs only
which

which could induce any man to divulge it, as no profit could arife therefrom, nor felfifh view be gratified.—It was mentioned by divine lips as a crime not in nature: " What man is there of you, " whom if his fon afk for bread, will " give him a ftone; or if he afk a fifh, " will give him a ferpent?"—Then can there be a man fo iniquitous among mafons, as to guide the thief to fteal from his fick brother the medicine which fhould reftore his health? the balfam which fhould clofe his wounds? the cloathing which fhould fhield his trembling limbs from the feverity of the winter? the drink which fhould moiften his fainting lip? the bread which fhould fave his foul alive?

Such is the importance of our fecrecy: —were there no other ties upon our affections or confciences, than merely the fenfe of the injury we fhould do to the poor and the wretched, by a tranfgreffion of this rule, I am perfuaded it would be fufficient to lock up the tongue of every man who profeffeth himfelf to be a MASON.

LEC-

LECTURE XI.

Of Charity.

AS one of the principal characteriftics of a Mafon, in this lecture, I will treat of CHARITY.

I do not mean to make ftrictures on that modern error of indifcriminately difpenfing alms to all fuppliants, without regard to their real wants or real merits; whereby the hypocrite and knave often eat the bread which virtue in diftrefs ought to be relieved by.——This is a miftaken character of charity, in which fhe is too often abufed.——Though the bounties of benevolence and compaffion are given with a righteous wifh, yet they fhould be ruled by difcretion.

The

The antients uſed to depict the virtue
CHARITY, in the character of a goddeſs,
ſeated in a chair of ivory, with a golden
tire upon her head, ſet with precious
ſtones:—her veſture, like the light of
heaven, repreſented univerſal benevolence; her throne was unpolluted and
unſpotted by paſſions and prejudices;
and the gems of her fillet repreſented
the ineſtimable bleſſings which flowed
variouſly from her bounty.

They alſo repreſented the charities,
otherwiſe called the graces, under three
perſonages:—one of theſe was painted
with her back towards us, and her face
forward, as proceeding from us; and the
other two with their faces towards us, to
denote, that for one benefit done we
ſhould receive double thanks:—they were
painted naked, to intimate that good offices ſhould be done without diſſembling
and hypocriſy:—they were repreſented
young, to ſignify that the remembrance
of benefits ſhould never wax old:—and
alſo laughing, to tell us that we ſhould
do good to others with chearfulneſs and
ala-

alacrity.—They were reprefented linked together, arm in arm, to inftruct us that one kindnefs fhould prompt another; fo that the knot and bond of love fhould be indiffoluble.—The poets tell us, that they ufed to wafh themfelves in the fountain Acidalius, becaufe benefits, gifts, and good-turns ought to be fincere and pure, and not bafe, fordid, and counterfeit.

CHARITY, in the works of moralifts, is defined to be the love of our brethren, or a kind of brotherly affection one to-wards another.—The rule and ftandard that this habit is to be examined and re-gulated by among chriftians, is the love we bear to ourfelves, or that the Me-diator bore towards us;—that is, it muft be unfeigned, conftant, and out of no other defign than their happinefs.

Such are the general fentiments which the antients entertained of this virtue, and what the modern moralifts and chrif-tians define it to be at this day.

In what character CHARITY fhould be received among mafons, is now my
purpofe

purpofe to define, as it ftands limited to
our own fociety.*

As being fo limited, we are not through
that channel fubject to be impofed on by
falfe pretences; and are certain of the
proper and merited adminiftration of it.
It is hence to be hoped, that it exifts
with us without diffembling or hypocrify,
and lives in fincerity and truth :—that benefits

---

* The principles which alone fhould attend a
candidate for initiation to our fociety, are pathe-
tically reprefented in the following pfalm.

PSALM XV.

1. " Lord, who fhall abide in thy tabernacle?
" who fhall abide in thy holy hill ?"

2. " He that walketh uprightly and worketh
" righteonfnefs, and fpeaketh the truth in his
" heart.'

3. " He that backbiteth not with his tongue,
" nor doth evil to his neighbour; nor taketh up a
" reproach againft his neighbour."

4. " In whofe eyes a vile perfon is contemned ;
" but he honoureth them that fear the Lord : he
" that fweareth to his own hurt and changeth not."

5. " He that putteth not out his money to
" ufury, nor taketh reward againft the innocent.
" —He that doeth thefe things fhall never be
" moved."

nefits received imprefs a lively degree of
gratitude and affection on the minds of
mafons, as their bounties fhould be beftowed with chearfulnefs, and unac-
quainted with the frozen finger of reluc-
tance:—the benevolence of our fociety
fhould be fo mutual and brotherly, that
each ought to 'endeavour to render good
offices, as readily as he would receive
them.*

N   In

---

* " The mifplacing of a benefit is-worfe than
" the not receiving of it ; for the one is another
" man's fault, but the other is mine. The error
" of the giver does oft times excufe the ingrati-
" tude of the receiver ; for a favour ill-placed is
" rather a profufion than a benefit. It is the moft
" fhameful of loffes, an inconfiderate bounty. I
" will chufe a man of integrity, fincere, confide-
" rate, grateful, temperate, well-natured, neither
" covetous nor fordid; and when I have obliged
" fuch a man, though not worth a groat in the
" world, I have gained my end. If we give only
" to receive, we lofe the faireft objects for our
" charity; the abfent, the fick, the captive, and
" the needy."
                              Seneca of Benefits.

" The rule is, we are to give as we would re-
" ceive, chearfully, quickly, and without hefita-
                              " tion :

In order to exercise this virtue, both
in the character of masons and in common life, with propriety, and agreeable
to such principles, we should forget every
obligation but affection; for otherwise it
were to confound charity with duty.—
The feelings of the heart ought to direct
the hand of CHARITY.—To this purpose we should be divested of every idea
of superiority, and estimate ourselves as
being of the same rank and race of men:
—in this disposition of mind we may be
susceptible of those sentiments which
CHARITY delighteth in, to feel the
woes and miseries of others with a ge-
nuine and true sympathy of soul:—COM-
PASSION

" tion ; for there is no grace in a benefit that
" sticks to the fingers.   A benefit should be made
" acceptable by all possible means, even to the
" end that the receiver, who is never to forget it,
" may bear it in his mind with satisfaction."

The same.

" It is not the value of the present, but the be-
" nevolence of the mind, that we are to consider:
" that which is given with pride and ostentation,
" is rather an ambition than a bounty."

The same.

PASSION is of heavenly birth;—it is one of the firſt characteriſtics of humanity.—Peculiar to our race, it diſtinguiſhes us from the reſt of creation.*

---

* 1 Corinth. chap. xiii.

Ver 1. " Though I ſpeak with the tongues of " men and of angels, and have not charity, I am " become as founding braſs, or a tinkling cymbal.

" 2. And though I have the gift of prophecy, " and underſtand all myſteries, and all know- " ledge; and though I have all faith, ſo that I " could remove mountains, and have not charity, " I am nothing.

" 3. And though I beſtow all my goods to feed " the poor, and though I give my body to be " burned, and have not charity, it profiteth me " nothing.

" 4. Charity ſuffereth long, and is kind; cha- " rity envieth not; charity vaunteth not itſelf, is " not puffed up.

" 5. Doth not behave itſelf unſeemly, ſeeketh " not her own, is not eaſily provoked, thinketh " no evil.

" 6. Rejoiceth not in iniquity, but rejoiceth in " the truth.

" 7. Beareth all things, believeth all things, " hopeth all things, endureth all things.

" 8. Charity never faileth: but whether there " be

He whofe bofom is locked up againft compaffion is a Barbarian;—his manners muft be brutal—his mind gloomy and morofe—and his paffions as favage as the beafts of the foreft.

What kind of man is he, who full of opulence, and in whofe hand abundance overflows, can look on virtue in diftrefs, and merit in mifery, without pity?—Who could behold without tears, the defolate and forlorn eftate of a WIDOW, who in early

---

" be prophecies, they fhall fail; whether there be
" tongues, they fhall ceafe; whether there be
" knowledge, it fhall vanifh away.
" 9. For we know in part, and we prophefy in
" part.
" 10. But when that which is perfect is come,
" then that which is in part fhall be done away.
" 11. " When I was a child, I fpake as a child,
" I underftood as a child, I thought as a child
" but when I became a man, I put away childifh
" things.
12. " For now we fee through a glafs, darkly;
" but then face to face : now I know in part;
" but then fhall I know, even as alfo I am known.
13. " And now abideth faith, hope, charity,
" thefe three; but the greateft of thefe is charity."

early life, having been brought up in
the bosom of a tender mother, without
knowing care, and without tasting of
necessity, was not befitted for adversity;
—whose soul was pure as innocence, and
full of honor;—whose mind had been
brightned by erudition under an indul-
gent father;—whose youth, untutored in
the school of sorrows, had been flattered
with the prospect of days of prosperity
and plenty;—one, who at length, by the
cruel adversity of winds and seas, with
her dying husband, is wrecked in total de-
struction and beggary; driven by ill fortune, from peace and plenty; and from
the bed of ease, changes her lot to the
dank dunghill, for the relief of her wea-
riness and pain;—grown meagre with
necessity, and sick with woe;—at her
bosom hanging her famished infant,
draining off the dregs of parental life,
for sustenance; bestowed from maternal
love—yielding existence to support the
babe.—Hard-hearted covetousness and
proud titles, can ye behold such an object, dry eyed?—Can avarice grasp the
mite which should sustain such virtue?
—Can high life lift its supercilious brow

above

above fuch fcenes in human life ; above
fuch miferies fuftained by a fellow-creature ?—If perchance the voice of the unfortunate and wretched widow is heard
in complainings, when wearying PATI-
ENCE and relaxing RESIGNATION
breathes a figh, whilft modefty forbids
her fupplication ; is not the groan, the
figh, more pathetic to your ear, you rich
ones, than all the flattering petitions of a
cringing knave, who touches your vanity
and tickles your follies ; extorting from
your very weakneffes, the proftituted portion of CHARITY.—Perhaps the fatal
hour's at hand, when confolation is required to clofe the laft moments of this
unfortunate one's life :—can the man ab-
forbed in pleafure roll his chariot wheels
beyond the fcene of forrow without compaffion, and without pity fee the laft con-
vulfion and the deadly gaze which paint
mifery upon the features of an expiring
faint!—If angels weep in heaven, they
weep for fuch:—if they can know contempt, they feel it for the wealthy, who
beftow not of their fuperfluities, and
fnatch not from their vices what would
gladden fouls funk in the woes of worldly
adver-

adverſity.—The eyes of cherubims view
with delight the exerciſe of ſuch benevolence as forms the character of the good
Samaritan:—ſaints touch their golden
lyres, to hymn HUMANITY's fair hiſtory
in realms of bliſs; and approbation ſhines
upon the countenance divine of OMNI-
PRESENCE, when a man is found in
the exerciſe of virtue.

What ſhould that human wretch be
called, who, with premeditated cruelty
and avarice, deviſes miſchief whilſt he is
conſcious of his neighbour's honeſty;—
whilſt he ſees him induſtriouſly, day by
day, labouring with ſweaty brow and
weary limbs, toiling with chearfulneſs for
bread,—on whoſe exerted labour, an affectionate and virtuous wife and healthy
children, crowding his narrow hearth
with naked feet, depend for ſuſtenance;
—whilſt he perceives him, with integrity
more than human, taking ſcrupu!ouſly
his own, and wronging no man for his
hunger or his wants;—whilſt he ſees him
with fatigued ſinews, lengthen out the
toil of induſtry, from morn to night with
unremitting ardor, ſinging to elude re-

N 4   pining,

pining, and fmoothing his anxieties and pain with hope, that he fhall reward his wearinefs by the overflowings of his wife's chearful heart, and with the fmiles of his feeding infants?—What muft he be, who knows fuch a man, and by his craft or avarice extorts unjuft demands, and brings him into beggary?—What muft he be, who fees fuch a man deprived by fire or water of all his fubftance, the habitation of his infants loft, and nothing left but nakednefs and tears,—and feeing this, affords the fufferer no relief?—Surely in nature few fuch wretches do exift! but if fuch be, it is not vain prefumption to proclaim, that like accurfed Cain, they are diftinguifhed as the outcaft of God's mercies, and are left on earth to live a life of punifhment.

The objects of true CHARITY, are MERIT and VIRTUE in diftrefs;—perfons who are incapable of extricating themfelves from misfortunes which have overtaken them in old age;—induftrious men, from inevitable accidents and acts of Providence rufhed into ruin;—widows left furvivors of their hufbands, by whofe
labours

labours they subsisted;—orphans in tender years left naked to the world.

What the claims of such, on the hand of charity, when you compare them to the miscreants who infest the doors of every dwelling with their importunities; wretches wandering from their homes, shewing their distortions and their sores to prompt compassion; with which ill-gotten gains, in concert with thieves and vagabonds, they revel away the hours of night which conceals their iniquities and vices.

CHARITY, when misapplied, loses her titles, and instead of being adorned with the dress of virtue, assumes the insignificance, the bells and feathers of folly.

LEC.

L E C T U R E XII.

On Brotherly Love.

I Shall treat of BROTHERLY LOVE, in this lecture, in that light which folely appertains to mafons.

The neceffity there is for the exertion of brotherly regard among mafons in the lodge, is obvious to every one:— PEACE, REGULARITY, and DECORUM are indifpenfible duties here:—all the fire of refentment, and remembrance of injuries, fhould be forgotten; and that cordiality ought to be warm among us, which brings with it chearfulnefs and rejoicing:—the true worfhipers of the Deity, men who held juft notions of the principles of nature, in the times of barbarous

igno-

ignorance, durſt not publicly practiſe the
one, or promulgate the other:—but happy
is our eſtate, in this lettered age and this
land of liberty, we profeſs our ſentiments
with freedom, and without fear; we exerciſe our religious principles under a full
toleration; and as ſocial beings we aſſemble
in the lodge, to enjoy the pleaſures of
friendſhip, and the breathings of true
benevolence without alloy.

After the buſineſs of the lodge is diſ-
patched, we are met together to open
out the chearfulneſs of our hearts without guile; for here are no tale-bearers,
cenſors, or revilers among us;—our lodge
is ſacred to SILENCE:—hence we may
ſay figuratively, " it is ſituate in the ſe-
" cret places, where the cock holdeth
" not his watch, where the voice of rail-
" ing reacheth not, where brawling, as
" the intemperate wrath of women, can-
" not be heard."

Without ſuſpicion of being betrayed in
our words, or enſnared in the openneſs
of our dealings, our mirth here is un-
diſguiſed, is governed by PRUDENCE,
tem-

tempered with LOVE, and cloathed in
CHARITY:—thus it ftandeth void of
offence:—no malicious mind warps innocent expreffions to wicked conftructions,
or interprets unmeaning jefts into far-
cafms or fatyres; but as every fentiment
flows full of benevolence, fo every ear
here, is attuned to the ftrain, in harmo-
nious concord, and taftes the pleafures of
feftivity fo pure, that they bear our re-
flections, in the morning, without remorfe.

Peace, regularity, and decorum, which
I faid were indifpenfible duties here, are
not the offspring of controul, or the iffue
of authority ; but a voluntary fervice,
which every man brings to the lodge.

There are feafons indeed, in which
authority is properly exercifed;—man is
frail;—the moft prudent may fometimes
deviate:—it was a maxim of the antient
philofophers, that " to err was human;"
therefore in the lodge there ought to be
a conftant governor, who fhould reftrain
the improprieties which may creep in
among us, by any brother coming here
after an intemperance in liquor.

Another

Another degree of brotherly love which fhould prevail here, is to hear the petitions of every member of this fociety with tendernefs and attention.—Where there is at any time a brother of our community fick or in diftrefs, the cafe of his calamities fhould come here reprefented by a brother, who will neither deceive us, nor hold back any part of his merits;—and the lodge muft teftify all due regard, by receiving the petition patiently, and giving relief according to the deferts.

The moft material part of that brotherly love which fhould fubfift among us mafons, is that of fpeaking well of each other to the world:—more efpecially it is expected of every member of this fraternity, that he fhould not traduce his brother.—Calumny and flander are deteftable crimes againft fociety.—Nothing can be viler than to traduce a man behind his back; it is like the villainy of an affaffin, who has not virtue enough to give his adverfary the means of felf-defence; but lurking in darknefs, ftabs

him

him whilft he is unarmed, and unfufpicious of an enemy.

Of this crime, the much-admired poet
Shakefpear has given a juft defcription.

" The man who fteals my purfe, fteals trafh ;
" 'Twas mine, 'tis his, and may be flave to thoufands:
" But he who pilfers from me my good name,
" Robs me of that which not enriches him,
" But makes me poor indeed."

Calumny has this direful confequence,
that it carries with it not a momentary
effect only, but endures for time un-
counted.—The wickednefs of the world
is fuch, that it is greedy of fcandal ; and
when once the voice of defamation hath
uttered its poifon, like a peftilence it
fmites and contaminates;—it fpreads jea-
loufies in families, divifion and wrath
among friends, urges fathers againft children, and brother againft brother.—When
once the pernicious tale gets birth, it
cannot be recalled ; and thence the finner's penitence is not capable of expiation: for the evil confequences may lay
dormant in the womb of futurity, and
become an intail of forrow on the third
and fourth generation of him that is in-
jured

jured.—What malice and mifchief, what
infernal difpofition, muft actuate the mind
which is capable of defaming the innocent!—there is no crime of which fuch a
wretch might not be the perpetrator;—
againft fuch a villain there is no armour
for defence;—he affaults the naked and
unfufpicious, and like the contagion of
fome horrid difeafe, he fmiteth whilft the
victim fleeps.—Juftice is difarmed againft
fuch a finner, as concealment is his fafe-
guard, and only the eye of heaven difcovers his iniquity.

It is not only expected of mafons, that
they fhould, with a confcientious foul, re-
refrain from evil-fpeaking; but alfo, that
they fhould fpeak well of each other.

To give a man his juft and due character, is fo eafy a duty, that it is not
poffible for a benevolent mind to avoid it;
—it is a degree of common juftice which
honefty itfelf prompts one to.—It is not
enough that we refrain from flander; but
it is required of mafons that they fhould
fpeak gracioufly and with affection, with-
holding nothing that can be uttered to a
brother's

brother's praife or good name with truth.
—What a pleafure doth it give the heart,
feeling benevolent difpofitions, to give
praifes where due.—There is a felfifh joy
in good fpeaking, as felf-approbation fuc-
ceeds it.—Befides, the breaft of fuch a
man feels enlarged, whilft he utters the
praife due to his neighbour; and he ex-
periences all the fineft fenfations of love,
whilft he moves others to the fame object
of his regard.

The neutral difpofition, frigid and re-
ferved, neither fpeaks good nor evil;—
but the man tafting brotherly love, is
warm to commend.—It is an eafy and
cheap means of beftowing good gifts and
working good works;—for by a juft
praife to induftry, you recommend the
induftrious man to thofe to whom he
might never be known, and thereby en-
large his credit and his trade.—By a juft
commendation of merit, you may open
the paths of advancement through thofe
whofe power might never have been petitioned.—By a proper praife of genius and
art, you may roufe the attention of thofe
patrons to whom the greateft defervings
might

might have remained a secret. It is a degree of juftice which every man has a right to, from his brother, that his virtues be not concealed.

To fhroud the imperfections of · our friend, and cloak his infirmities, is chriftian-like, and charitable, confequently befitting a mafon:—even the truth fhould not be told at all times; for where we cannot approve, we fhould pity in filence. —What pleafure or profit can there arife by expofing the fecrets of a brother?— To exhort him, is virtuous;—to revile him, is inhuman;—and to fet him out as an object of ridicule, is infernal.

From hence we muft neceffarily determine, that the duty of a good man leads to work the works of benevolence; and his heart is touched with joy, whilft he acts within her precepts.

Let us therefore be ftedfaft and immoveable in our ordinances, that we be proved to have A TONGUE OF GOOD REPORT.

L E C T U R E XIII.

On the Occupations *of* Masons.

IN my former lectures I have declared it to be my opinion, that MASONS, in the present state of MASONRY, were never a body of architects.—By the book of constitutions published by authority, we see no grand communication held in form, till of very late date: neither is there any evidence therein to contradict the propositions I have laid down.—The succession therein described, is by no means to be accepted and understood in a literal sense; but as a pedigree or chronological table of the servants of the Deity, working in the duties of righteousness.

I ground

I ground my judgment of the nature of our profeſſion on our ceremonials, and am convinced they have not their relation to building and architecture, but are emblematical, and imply moral, ſpiritual, and religious tenets.—It appears to me ſelf-evident, that the ſituation of the lodge, and its ſeveral parts, are copied after the tabernacle and temple, and are repreſentative of the univerſe, implying that the univerſe is the temple in which the Deity is every where preſent; our mode of teaching the principles of our profeſſion, is derived from the Druids; our maxims of morality, from Pythagoras; our chief emblems, originally from Egypt; to Baſilides we owe the ſcience of Abrax, and the characters of thoſe emanations of the Deity which we have adopted, and which are ſo neceſſary for the maintenance of a moral ſociety.—I am induced to believe, that our preſent ceremonies were more generally taught, and more candidates were initiated therein, on the opening of the cruſades, than in any other æra, or on any other known occaſion.

O 2   The

The Englifh hiftorians agree, that in the reign of Henry the Second, and in the year 1188, at an interview between the Kings of England and France, attended by the prelates and nobility of both nations, the Archbifhop of Tyre pronounced fuch a melancholy account of Saladine's fuccefs in the Holy Land, and the miferies of the chriftians in that country, that the audience was greatly affected with the relation; and the two kings agreed to convert their whole attention to the relief of thofe adventurers. —They received the crofs from the hands of the archbifhop, refolving to go there in perfon; and their example was followed by Philip Count of Flanders, and a great number of the prelates and nobility there prefent:—A PLENARY INDULGENCE was publifhed in the pope's name, for all that would make a fair confeffion of their fins, and engage in the crufade:—the different nations affumed croffes of a different colour, and RULES AND ORDERS were eftablifhed for preventing RIOT, LUXURY, AND DISORDER on the enterprize.

Thefe

Thefe were the principal rules made for the regulation of the crufaders.—We may conjecture thefe religious campaigns being over, that men initiated in the myfteries of mafonry, and engaged and inrolled under thofe rules and orders, which were eftablifhed for the conduct of the nations in the holy war, would form themfelves into lodges, and keep up their focial meetings when returned home, in commemoration of their adventures and mutual good offices in Paleftine, and for the propagation of that knowledge into which they had been initiated.

As a further argument that builders and architects were not the original members of our fociety, the MASONS of the city of London obtained their incorporation and charter in the reign of King Henry the Fifth, in or about the year 1419; they taking on themfelves the name of FREE MASONS.—By their charter they are governed by a mafter and two wardens, with twenty-five affiftants.—Of this incorporated body, fixty-five are of the livery of London.

O 3

It

It has never been pretended, that the
fociety of FREE AND ACCEPTED
MASONS have in any manner been connected, or much lefs have united themfelves, with the incorporated body of mafons enchartered; but on the contrary,
have kept themfelves totally apart.

It has been alledged, that in the reign
of King Henry the Sixth an obfolete law
was enacted, fetting forth, " that by the
" yearly congregations and confederacies
" made by mafons in their general affem-
" blies, the good courfe and effects of the
" ftatute of labourers were openly vio-
" lated and broken, and making the fu-
" ture holding of their chapters and con-
" gregations felony."

It is impoffible that this ftatute fhould
relate to any other perfons, than the incorporated body of working mafons;
who under an exclufive charter, by fecret combinations raifed the prices of their
labour, and prevented craftfmen of their
fraternity, not members of the charter,
from exercifing their trade within the
limits

limits of London; which might occasion a grievance worthy of parliamentary redress:—but in what manner the statutes of labourers could be affected by the associations of this fraternity of ours, is not in my power to comprehend. Our records give us no evidence of any such convocations, at the time mentioned.

By the charter of MASONS, they assumed the title of FREE MASONS, being intitled to the franchises of the city of London.

Why the title of FREE is annexed to our society, or that of ACCEPTED, I hope I may be allowed to conjecture was derived from the crusades.—There the volunteers entering into that service must be FREEMEN, born free, and not villains or under any vassallage; for it was not until long after the crusades, that vassallage and feudal services, together with the slavish tenures, were taken away.

They were intitled to the stile of ACCEPTED, under that PLENARY IN-

O 4   DUL-

DULGENCE which the pope publifhed, for all that would confefs their fins, and inlift in the enterprize of the holy war; whereby they were accepted and received into the bofom of the father of the church. —Some authors have prefumed to tell us, that it was the original defign of the chriftian powers, in their enterprize in the Holy Land, to rebuild the temple at Jerufalem ; but I cannot difcover any good authority for this affertion.—In modern mafonry it is given as a principle, why our dedication of lodges is made to ST JOHN, that the mafons who engaged to conquer the Holy Land, chofe that faint for their patron—I fhould be forry to appropriate the Balfarian fect of chriftians of St John, as an explanation of this principle;—ST JOHN obtains our dedication, as being the proclaimer of that falvation which was at hand, by the coming of Chrift; and we, as a fet of religious affembling in the true faith, commemorate the proclamations of the Baptift.—In the name of ST JOHN THE EVANGELIST, we acknowledge the teftimonies which he gives, and the divine λόγος, which he makes manifeft.—
But

But to return to the fubject of the crufaders.

It is probable that the fame enthufiaftic
fpirit which engaged men to enter into
the crufades, at the vaft expence and ha-
zard which hiftory defcribes, alfo led
them into as enormous a folly in the
building of religious houfes:—during the
reign of Henry the Second, when the
Englifh firft engaged in the holy war,
there were not lefs than one hundred and
eleven abbeys, nunneries, and religious
houfes founded in this kingdom;—during the reign of Richard the Firft, eigh-
teen;—and during the reign of Henry
the Third, forty: which fhews the religious infatuation which had totally over-
run the minds of the people in thofe
reigns.—The Ecclefiaftics, in imitation of
the works of Solomon, might become
the mafters of thofe works, and fuperin-
tend and conduct the labours of the inferior fect of haly-wark-folk; that by
acceptable hands fuch pious works might
be conducted, and from whence the ignorant and profane might be rejected,
like the Samaritans:—thefe might affume
the

the honorary title of MASONS, which from vulgar acceptation, would naturally confound them with ordinary mechanics.

In the Angla-Norman Antiquities, it is said of FREE MASONS, that they were an affociation of religious, who engaged in the founding and erecting of churches and religious houfes in Paleftine. —I have already mentioned the religious fect who were really architects and builders of churches, the haly-wark-folk, with no fmall degree of refpect : they were a body of men fubfifting before the crufades:—they were maintained by the church, under which they held lands for the fervice of erecting and repairing churches, and for the guarding of the fepulchres of faints.—It is not improbable, that when the rage of holy works and holy wars and the defire of Paleftine fired the minds of all Europe, but a body of thofe people might embark in the enterprize, and be tranfported thither to build churches, for the better planting or propagating the chriftian doctrine, or to guard and maintain the holy fepulchre.— I would be ready at all times to admit
thefe

thefe emigrants might poffefs fome rules
and ceremonies for initiation peculiar to
themfelves, fo far as the bearers of burthens were admitted under Solomon in
the building at Jerufalem, and that they
might retain their fingular maxims and
principles in fecrecy:—and it may alfo be
àdmitted, that in honor of that gradation
of mafonry and of their profeffion, they
fhould claim the greateft antiquity, from
Solomon's temple at leaft:—they might
even be more than a collateral branch of
the FREE AND ACCEPTED MASONS,
as I have before admitted, and be initiated in the myfteries of mafonry, their
occupation being in no wife incompatible
with our profeffion, and they might be
known and diftinguifhed by the title of
OPERATIVE MASONS, as the Effenes
were divided into theoricks and practicks:
—but from the writings of the author of
the Angla-Norman Antiquities, I am convinced he was not a FREE AND ACCEP-
TED MASON himfelf; and as the fecrecy
of that fociety had attracted the attention
of many, who as their curiofity was exercifed, raifed conjectures on the name of
mafons, to difcover their origin and principles,

ciples, or to reconcile their own opinions: from whence, nothing was more likely to ftrike the attention of an hiftorian, than this body of men; the haly-wark-folk rambling in Paleftine were to his purpofe.

Were we claimants only of the title of mechanics, we might have chofe as an-tient and a more honorable branch of the arts or fciences;—we might have fubfti-tuted geometry to a more worthy duty, and have honored our Maker in fome profeffion more expreffive of our fenfe of his power and dignity.

Our ORIGIN in this country is thought to be from the PHOENICI-ANS who came here with the Tyrian Hercules, and introduced the doctrines of HAM and the AMONIAN rites, together with the HEBREW CUS-TOMS; and afterwards the emigrants from the Holy Land, who taught us the rules inftituted by SOLOMON at the temple of Jerufalem; and finally, the propagators of the chriftian doctrine, who brought with them the principles of the
Mafter's

Mafter's Order, and taught the converted thofe facred myfteries which are
typical of the chriftian faith, and pro-
feffional of the hope of the refurrection of
the body and the life of regeneration. Yet
I fear few among us are equal to the character we have affumed. Our LODGES
are not now appropriated to WORSHIP
and RELIGIOUS CEREMONIES; we
meet as A SOCIAL SOCIETY, inclined
to acts of benevolence, and fuffer the
more facred offices to reft unperformed.
—Whether this neglect is to our honor,
I prefume not to remonftrate; in our
PRESENT STATE profeffing ourfelves
FREE AND ACCEPTED MASONS.
We are totally fevered from architects,
and are become a fet of men working in
the duties of CHARITY, GOOD OF-
FICES, and BROTHERLY LOVE—
chriftians in religion—fons of liberty and
loyal fubjects:—we have adopted rules,
orders, emblems, and fymbols, which
enjoin us to live a life of morality:—we
have furnifhed our lodges with thofe
ftriking objects, which fhould at once intimate to us the mightinefs and wifdom
of

of God, the inftability of the affairs of
man, and the various viciffitudes in human life, and have fet before our eyes
preceptors of moral works; and to
ftrengthen our faith, we have enlightned
our lodge with the emblem of the Trinity.

It is well known to us, that there is
fcarce a ftate in Europe, in which our
fraternity have not formed a body.—The
wifdom of the antients would pafs abroad
into many regions, and thofe who had
affifted in the pious labours at Jerufalem,
would, like Pythagoras, teach the fciences
and myfteries which they profeffed, and
communicate the fyftem to which they
had been initiated;—religious men would
retain the doctrines and myfteries with
reverence, and with caution reveal them
to thofe they thought worthy to receive;
hence the original knowledge would pafs
into many countries:—but there is no
accounting for this univerfality of the fociety, upon the principles of architecture
and operative mafonry:—the rage of
church-building had not contaminated all
Europe as it did England; neither is there
any probable means to be deduced from
archi-

architecture and the practice of builders,
to account why in every tongue, and in
every kingdom, the ceremonials of being
made a mafon fhould be the fame.—If
the honor of architecture was all that was
to be regarded in the fociety, various
would be the devices by which the members in each nation would profefs it.—
As architecture, according to its prefent
orders, had its progrefs from Egypt and
Greece, fome nations would have borrowed fymbols and enfigns peculiar to
thofe people; or we fhould have had in
our ceremonies, or in our workings, fome
devices which might have diftinguifhed
to us the beauties, orders, ornaments,
proportions, or fymmetries, of fome or
all of the rules, modes, or orders of architecture, either from the plains of Shinar,
from Egypt, Jerufalem, Tadmore, or
Greece; or have retained fome geometrical problems, on which the general
principles of proportion in architecture
were grounded or demonftrated:—but
inftead of that, it is well known to us,
that there is nothing of that kind revealed. On the contrary, our myfteries are
totally abftracted from the rules of mechanics:

chanics : they are relative to religion and morality, and are conducive to pious works : they are unfurniſhed with any type, ſymbol, or character, but what appertains to demonſtrate the ſervants and devotees of the great Μεσυρανεω.

There is not an inſtance of the European ſtates uniting in any one enterprize, ſave the holy war; and from thence, we moſt rationally muſt conceive, the preſent number of maſons diſperſed over the face of Europe was principally derived. The Amonian rites are almoſt totally diſtinguiſhed, religious zeal has imbrued the ſword in carnage, and Europe has groaned under perſecutions; the Romans extirpated the Druids, chriſtians have glutted their cruel hands with ſlaughter, bigotry and enthuſiaſm in every age have reigned in bloodſhed.—By the cruſades, the number of our ſociety would be greatly augmented; the occaſion itſelf would revive the rules of maſonry, they being ſo well adapted to that purpoſe, and alſo profeſſional of the chriſtian faith, from whence ſprang the ſpirit of the enterprize.—After theſe purſuits ſubſided, bodies

bodies of men would be found in every country from whence the levies were called; and what would preferve the fociety in every ftate, even during the perfecutions of zealots, the Mafter Mafon's Order, under its prefent principles, is adapted to every fect of chriftians. It originated from the earlieft æra of chriftianity, in honor to, or in confeffion of, the religion and faith of chriftians, before the poifon of fectaries was diffufed over the church.

To the antient rules, deduced from Solomon, other laws, rules, and ordinances were added, upon the enterprizes of the crufaders, for the prevention of riot, luxury, and diforder; and for the maintaining that neceffary fubordination, which the command of fuch armies required. Many of thefe rules we retain in the conduct and government of our lodge, which can in no wife be deduced from any other original.

P   LEC

LECTURE XIV.

A Corollary.

I Shall now conclude thefe Lectures, with collecting into one view, the propofitions and maxims which have engaged my attention throughout the whole work; thereby to give a clear idea of the myfteries of mafonry, the progreffion and fpirit of its inftitution, origin, and prefent ftate.

I may have feemed prolix, and have filled my arguments or reprefentations with repetitions; but where that feeming impropriety takes place, it was neceffary to urge a pofition which contended with fome accepted error, prepoffeffion, or vulgar prejudice.

From

From the antient rites and ceremonies which I have laid before you, it will be eafy for you to trace the origins of our own, and to difcover the foundations on which our fociety was erected. It is evident they had their progrefs in the poftdeluvian world from Ham. I am under a neceffity fometimes to ufe terms of art, or expreffions which to others may not carry diftinct and clear images; but to my brethren, breathe an energy which flows from the united force of technical terms, fymbols, and hieroglyphics. When I fpeak of mafons under the denomination of a fociety, I mean mafons as embodied in lodges, according to the prefent manners in which fuch lodges are held.—Our antiquity is in our principles, maxims, language, learning, and religion:—thefe we derive from Eden, from the patriarchs, and from the fages of the eaft; all which are made perfect under the chriftian difpenfation.—The light and doctrines which we poffefs, are derived from the beginning of time, and have defcended through this long fucceffion of ages uncorrupted; but our modes and manners are deduced from the different

P 2   æras

æras of paradife, the building of the temple at Jerufalem, and the chriftian revelation.

I have explained to you, that the ftructure of the LODGE is a pattern of the univerfe, and that the firft entry of a inafon reprefents the firft worfhip of the true God.——We have retained the Egyptian fymbols of the SUN AND MOON, as the emblems of God's power, eternity, omniprefence, and benevolence; and thereby we fignify, that we are the children of light, and that the firft foundation of our profeffion, is the knowledge and adoration of the Almighty, Μεσυρανεω, who feateth himfelf in the centre of the heavens:——we derive from the Druids many of the Amonian rites; and I am bold to fay, that we retain more of the ceremonials and doctrines of the Druids, than is to be found in the whole world befides; and have faved from oblivion, many of their religious rites, in our initiation to the firft degree of mafonry, which otherwife would have flept in eternity. Thefe we feem to have mixed and tempered with the principles of the Effenes, who

who are a fect as antient as the departure
of the children of Ifrael out of Egypt.—
The philofophy of the Egyptians, and the
manners, principles, and cuftoms of the
Hebrews, were introduced to this land by
the Phœnicians, and make a part of our
profeffion, fo far as they are adapted to
the worfhip of NATURE'S GREAT AU-
THOR, unpolluted by idolatry.

We hold our grand feftival on the day
of ST JOHN, which is Midfummer-day;
in which we celebrate that feafon when
the fun is in its greateft altitude, and in
the midft of its prolific powers : the great
type of the omnipotence of the Deity.

The famous lawyer, Lord Cook, in his
Treatife on Littleton's Inftitutes, fays,
" Prudent antiquity did, for more folem-
" nity and better memory and obferva-
" tion of that which is to be done, ex-
" prefs fubftances under ceremonies."

I have pointed out to you, that the
FURNITURES of the LODGE are emblems excitive of morality and good government:—PRUDENCE fhiues in the
P 3   centre,

centre, or if you would apply this object
to more facred principles, it reprefents
the blazing ftar which conducted the
wife men to Bethlehem, and proclaimed
the prefence of the SON OF GOD. It
is here placed in your view, that you
may remember to work out the works of
falvation, which is at hand:—and that
you may pafs on in acts of ftrict propriety
with greater alacrity, the TASSALATA
or MOSAIC-WORK intimates to you,
the chequered diverfity and uncertainty
of human affairs; that you may not fet
your hearts on the things of this world,
but lay up your treafures where the ruft
cannot deface their polifh and luftre, neither can the moth defpoil the garment
for the wedding feaft.

To protect and fupport us under the
infirmities of nature, and lead us to the
paths of propriety, the BOOK OF TRUE
KNOWLEDGE is in the lodge;—the
MASTER circumfcribes you, as with
the fweep of the COMPASS; and the
SQUARE is your trial, whereby you
fhall prove the rectitude and uniformity
cf your manners.

In

In my next Lecture I demonſtrated to you, that to be a worthy ſervant in the temple of God, you muſt be cloathed with INNOCENCE, that your ſervice may ſtand in approbation, and you may be accepted in heaven.—Our jewels are emblems of that good working in a moral mind which adorns the life of man; FAITH, CHARITY, AND UPRIGHT-NESS.

In the ſucceeding Lecture, I have led you to a diſcernment of the ſecond race of the ſervants of God, under the MO-SAIC LAW; the truth being ſtripped of the errors of idolatry.—This ſtage is a-dapted to the ſecond gradation of ma-ſonry.

I have argued for the propriety of our adopting GEOMETRY in this ſociety, as being a ſcience, from whence the mighty powers of God are revealed and demon-ſtrated to mankind.

Afterwards I attended to the eſtate of the worſhippers of the Deity, under the
P 4   cor-

corruptions of the houfe of Ifrael, and
under the rottennefs of the old law.—In
this affembly of chriftians, it is in no wife
requifite to attempt an argument on the
neceffity which there was upon earth for
a Mediator and Saviour for man:—in the
rubbifh, fuperftitions, ceremonials, and
filth of the Jewifh temple, the true worfhip of God was buried and confounded,
and INNOCENCE became only the ornaments of its monument.—Then it was
that the Divinity, looking down with an
eye of commiferation on the deplorable
ftate of man, in his mercy and love fent
us a Preceptor and Mediator, who fhould
teach to us the doctrine of regeneration,
and raife us from the fepulchre of fin, to
which the human race had refigned themfelves:—he gave to us the precepts of
that acceptable fervice, wherewith his
Father fhould be well pleafed: he made
the facrifice of expiation, and becoming
the firft-fruits of them that flept, mani-
fefted to mankind the refurrection of the
body and the life everlafting.—In the
MASTER'S ORDER this whole doctrine
is fymbolized, and the chriftian conduct
is by types prefented to us.

We

We MASONS have adopted three particular characteristics, SECRECY, CHARITY, AND BROTHERLY LOVE.— I have explained my sense of these three great duties, and of what especial import they are of to MASONS; or to men who have separated themselves from the rest of mankind, and professed they are servants of HIM WHO RULETH IN THE MIDST OF HEAVEN.

Lastly, I have attempted to examine into the origin of our society, and in many instances, wand'ring without evidence, I have been left to probability in conjecture only.—It doth not now seem material to us what our originals and predecessors were, if we occupy ourselves in the true SPIRIT OF MASONRY; in that divine spirit which inspired the patriarchs when they erected altars unto the Lord; if we are true servants to our king, faithful and true to our chartered liberties, christians in profession and in practice, and to each other, and mankind in general, affectionate and upright.

Whether

Whether MASONS were originally builders or religious, it matters not to us in this age:—comparing thefe works with the righteoufnefs to which I have exhorted you, the honor of the antiquity would be fwallowed up in the virtues of practice, and in the fplendor of that LIGHT OF ACCEPTATION, which at once proclaims to the world that we are fervants of the true God, who faves our fouls alive.

If our ceremonies mean not the matter which I have expreffed; if they imply not the moral and religious principles which I have endeavoured to unveil; I afk you, MASONS, what they do imply, import, or indicate?

Can we prefume fo many learned and noble perfonages would, for many fucceffive ages, have been fteady members of this fraternity, if the myfteries were unimportant, and the ceremonies unintelligible?—It cannot be;—take away their SPIRIT, and they become ridiculous.

Hath

Hath it been for ages a maxim or
foolifh fport, to induce men to a filly
fnare, in which the guide, having been
entrapped into ridicule, longs to laugh
at another for revenge?—It is too ridiculous to be prefumed.—Befides, if it was
only fo, the fnare might be formed and
ornamented with fimple things, and there
was no need to introduce facred matters
into the device.—This renders the conjecture fo abfurd, that it will bear no further animadverfions.

We MASONS profefs that we are
pilgrims in progreffion from the EAST.

The Almighty planted a garden in the
EAST, wherein he placed the perfection
of human nature, the firft man, full of
innocence and divine knowledge, and full
of honor, even bearing the image of God.

Learning had its firft progreffion from
the EAST after the flood : the Egyptians
were the firft devifers of the zodiac, and
the firft difcerners of the wifdom of the
great ARCHITECT OF THE WORLD
in

in the revolutions of the heavens : they were the firſt projectors of the ſcience of GEOMETRY.

In regard to the doctrine of our Saviour and the chriſtian revelation, it proceeded from the EAST.

The ſtar which proclaimed the birth of the Son of God, appeared in the EAST.

The EAST was an expreſſion uſed by the prophets to denote the Redeemer.

From thence it may well be conceived, that we ſhould profeſs our progreſs to be from thence; if we profeſs by being MASONS, that we are a ſociety of the ſervants of that Divinity, whoſe abode is with the Father coeternal, in the centre of the heavens.

But if we profeſs no ſuch matter, then why ſhould not we have alledged our progreſs to have been from the north, and the regions of chaos and darkneſs?

But

But I will now, my brethren, forbear all further argument, and clofe the labours of my year with a fincere exhortation, that you will continue to act in this fociety as upright and religious men;—that you will exert yourfelves in the promotion of its honor;—and let the wicked and ignorant revile never fo malicioufly, be ftrenuous in your duties, as MASONS and as BRETHREN :—exercife your benevolence with opennefs of heart, and your charity with cordiality, and not as hypocrites :—with attention endeavour to arrive at the utmoft knowledge of your PROFESSION, the end of which, I prefume to proclaim to you, is to work out THE WORKS OF RIGHTEOUSNESS.

THE END.

APPENDIX.

A LETTER *from the learned Mr* JOHN LOCKE, *to the Right Hon.* THOMAS *Earl of* PEMBROKE, *with an old* MANUSCRIPT *on the Subject of* FREE-MASONRY.

MY LORD,   6th *May,* 1696.

I Have at length, by the help of Mr Collins, procured a copy of that M. S. in the Bodleian library, which you were fo curious to fee : and, in obedience to your Lordfhip's commands, I herewith fend it to you. Moft of the notes annexed to it, are what I made yefterday for the reading of my lady Mafham, who is become fo fond of mafonry, as to fay, that fhe now more than ever wifhes herfelf a man, that fhe might be capable of admiffion into the fraternity.

The M. S. of which this is a copy, appears to be about 160 years old; yet (as your Lordfhip will obferve by the title) it is itfelf a copy of one yet more ancient by about 100 years : for the original is faid to have been the hand-writing of

K.

K. Henry VI. Where that prince had it
is at prefent an uncertainty; but it feems
to me to be an examination (taken perhaps before the king) of fome one of the
brotherhood of mafons; among whom
he entered himfelf, as it is faid, when he
came out of his minority, and thence-
forth put a ftop to a perfecution that had
been raifed againft them : But I muft not
detain your Lordfhip longer by my pre-
face from the thing itfelf.

I know not what effect the fight of this
old * paper may have upon your Lordfhip; but for my own part I cannot deny,
that it has fo much raifed my curiofity,
as to induce me to enter myfelf into the
fraternity, which I am determined to do
(if I may be admitted) the next time I go
to London, and that will be fhortly.

I am,
My Lord,
Your Lordship's *moft obedient,*
And moft humble fervant,
JOHN LOCKE.

---

* The paper alluded to by Mr Locke, is the
immediately following one.

CERTAYNE QUESTYONS,

WYTH

ANSWERES TO THE SAME,

CONCERNING THE

MYSTERY of MACONRYE;

Writene by the hande of kynge HENRYE,
the fixthe of the name,

And faythfullye copyed by me (1) JOHAN
LEYLANDE, *Antiquarius,*

By the commaunde of his (2) Highneſſe.

They be as followethe,

QUEST. WHAT mote ytt be? (3)
ANSW. Ytt beeth the ſkyllé
of nature, the underſtondynge of the
myghte that ys hereynne, and its fondrye
werckynges; fonderlyche, the ſkylle of
rectenyngs, of waightes and metynges,
and the treu manere of faconnynge al
thynges for mannes uſe; headlye, dwel-
lynges, and buyldynges of alle kindes,
Q   and

and al odher thynges that make gudde
to manne.

QUEST. Where dyd ytt begyne?

ANSW. Ytt dyd begynne with the (4)
fyrfte menne in the efte, whych were
before the (5) ffyrfte manne of the wefte,
and comynge weftlye, ytt hathe broughte
herwyth alle comfortes to the wylde and
comfortleffe.

QUEST. Who dyd brynge ytt weftlye?

ANSW. The (6) Venetians, whoo be-
ynge grate merchaundes, comed ffyrfte
ffromme the efte ynn Venetia, for the
commodytye of marchaundyfynge beithe
efte and wefte, bey the redde and myd-
dlelonde fees.

QUEST. Howe comede ytt yn Engelonde?

ANSW. Peter Gower (7) a Grecian,
journeyedde ffor kunnynge yn Egypte,
and yn Syria, and yn everyche londe
whereas the Venetians hadde plauntedde
maconrye, and wynnynge entraunce yn
al lodges of maconnes, he lerned muche,
and retournedde, and woned yn Grecia
magna (8) wackfynge, and becommynge
a myghtye (9) wyfeacre, and greatlyche
renowned, and her he framed a grate
lodge at Groton (10), and maked many
maconnes,

maconnes, fome whereoffe dyd journeye
yn Fraunce, and maked manye maconnes,
wherefromme, yn proceffe of tyme, the
arte paffed yn Engelonde.

QUEST. Dothe maconnes difcouer there
artes unto odhers?

ANSW. Peter Gower, whenne he journeyedde to lernne, was ffyrfte (11) made,
and anonne techedde; evenne foe fhulde
all odhers beyn recht. Nathelefs (12) maconnes hauethe always yn everyche tyme,
from tyme to tyme, communycatedde to
mannkynde foche of ther fecrettes as gene-
rallyche myghte be ufefulle; they haueth
keped backe foche allein as fhulde be
harmefulle yff they comed yn euylle
haundes, oder foche as ne mighte be
holpynge wythouten the techynges to be
joynedde herwythe in the lodge, oder
foche as do bynde the freres more ftronge-
lyche together, bey the proffytte and commodytye comynge to the confrerie her-
fromme.

QUEST. Whatte artes haueth the maconnes techedde mankynde?

ANSW. The artes (13) agricultura, ar-
chitectura, aftronomia, geometria, nu-
meres,

meres, mufica, poefie, kymiftrye, govern-
mente, and relygyonne.

QUEST. Howe commethe maconnes
more teachers than odher menne?

ANSW. The hemfelfe haueth allein in
(14) arte of fyndinge neue artes, whyche
arte the ffyrfte maconnes receaued from
Godde; by the whyche they fyndethe
what artes hem plefethe, and the treu
way of techynge the fame. Whatt odher
menne doethe ffynde out, ys onelyche bey
chaunce, and therfore but lytel I tro.

QUEST. What dothe the maconnes
concele and hyde?

QUEST. They concelethe the art of
ffyndynge neue artes, and thattys for here
own proffyte, and (15) preife: They
concelethe the art of kepynge (16) fecrettes, thatt fo the worlde mayeth no-
thinge concele from them. They concelethe the art of wunderwerckynge, and of
forefayinge thynges to comme, thatt fo
thay fame artes may not be ufedde of the
wyckedde to an euyell ende; thay alfo
concelethe the (17) arte of chaunges, the
wey of wynnynge the facultye (18) of
Abrac, the fkylle of becommynge gude
and parfyghte wythouten the holpynges

of

of fere and hope; and the univerſelle (19) longage of maconnes.

QUEST. Wyll he teche me thay ſame artes?

ANSW Ye ſhalle be techedde yff ye be warthye, and able to lerne.

QUEST. Dothe all maconnes kunne more then odher menne?

ANSW. Not ſo. Thay onlyche haueth recht and occaſyonne more then odher menne to kunne, butt manye doeth fale yn capacity, and manye more doth want induſtrye, thatt ys perneceſſarye for the gaynynge all kunnynge.

QUEST. Are maconnes gudder menne then odhers?

ANSW. Some maconnes are not ſo ver-tuous as ſome other menne; but, yn the moſte parte, thay be more gude than they woulde be yf thay war not maconnes.

QUEST. Doth maconnes love eidther odher myghtylye as beeth ſayde?

ANSW. Yea verylyche, and yt may not odherwiſe be : For gude menne and treu, kennynge eidher odher to be ſoche, doeth always love the more as thay be more gude.

Here endethe the queſtyonnes, and awnſweres.

NOTES

N O T E S

A N D

O B S E R V A T I O N S,

O N T H E

FOREGOING QUESTIONS.

By Mr. LOCKE.

(1) JOHN LEYLANDE was appointed by Henry VIII. at the diffolution of monafteries, to fearch for, and fave fuch books and records as were valuable among them. He was a man of great labour and induftry.

(2) HIS HIGHNESSE, meaning the faid king Henry VIII. Our kings had not then the title of majefty.

(3) What

(3) What mote ytt be?] That is, what may this myftery of mafonry be? The anfwer imports, that it confifts in natural, mathematical, and mechanical knowledge. Some part of which (as appears by what follows) the mafons pretend to have taught the reft of mankind, and fome part they ftill conceal.

(4) (5) Fyrfte menne yn the efte, &c.] It fhould feem by this that mafons believe there were men in the eaft before Adam, who is called " the ffyrfte manne of the wefte;" and that arts and fciences began in the eaft. Some authors of great note for learning have been of the fame opinion; and it is certain that Europe and Africa (which, in refpect to Afia, may be called weftern countries) were wild and favage, long after arts and politenefs of manners were in great perfection in China, and the Indies.

(6) The Venetians, &c.] In the times of monkifh ignorance it is no wonder that the Phenicians fhould be miftaken for the Venetians. Or, perhaps, if the people

were

were not taken one for the other, fimilitude of found might deceive the clerk
who firft took down the examination.
The Phenicians were the greateft voyagers
among the ancients, and were in Europe
thought to be the inventors of letters,
which perhaps they brought from the eaft
with other arts.

(7) Peter Gower.] This muft be another miftake of the writer. I was puz-
zled at firft to guefs who Peter Gower
fhould be, the name being perfectly
Englifh; or how a Greek fhould come
by fuch a name: But as foon as I thought
of Pythagoras, I could fcarce forbear fmi-
ling, to find that philofopher had undergone a metempfycofis he never dreamt
of. We need only confider the French
pronunciation of his name, Pythagore,
that is Petagore, to conceive how eafily
fuch a miftake might be made by an un-
learned clerk. That Pythagoras travelled
for knowledge into Egypt, &c. is known
to all the learned; and that he was initiated into feveral different orders of priefts,
who in thofe days kept all their learning
fecret from the vulgar, is as well known.
Pytha-

Pythagoras alfo made every geometrical theorem a fecret, and admitted only fuch to the knowledge of them, as had firft undergone a five years filence. He is fuppofed to be the inventor of the 47th propofition of the firft book of Euclid, for which, in the joy of his heart, it is faid he facrificed a hecatomb. He alfo knew the true fyftem of the world, lately revived by Copernicus; and was certainly a moft wonderful man. See his life by DION HAL.

(8) GRECIA MAGNA, a part of Italy formerly fo called, in which the Greeks had fettled a large colony.

(9) Wyfeacre.] This word at prefent fignifies fimpleton, but formerly had a quite contrary meaning. Weifager, in the old Saxon, is philofopher, wifeman, or wizard, and having been frequently ufed ironically, at length came to have a direct meaning in the ironical fenfe. Thus, Duns Scotus, a man famed for the fubtilty and acutenefs of his under-ftanding, has, by the fame method of irony,

irony, given a general name to modern dunces.

(10) Groton.] Groton is the name of a place in England. The place here meant is Crotona, a city of Grecia Magna, which in the time of Pythagoras was very populous.

(11) Fyrſte made.] The word MADE I ſuppoſe has a particular meaning among the maſons: perhaps it ſignifies, initiated.

(12) Maconnes haueth communycatedde, &c.] This paragraph hath ſomething remarkable in it. It contains a juſtification of the ſecrecy ſo much boaſted of by maſons, and ſo much blamed by others; aſſerting that they have in all ages diſcovered ſuch things as might be uſeful, and that they conceal ſuch only as would be hurtful either to the world or themſelves. What theſe ſecrets are, we ſee afterwards.

(13) The artes, agricultura, &c.] It ſeems a bold pretence this of the maſons,
that

that they have taught mankind all thefe arts. They have their own authority for it; and I know not how we fhall dif-prove them. But what appears moſt odd is, that they reckon religion among the arts.

(14) Arte of ffyndinge neue artes.] The art of inventing arts, muſt certainly be a moſt ufeful art. My lord Bacon's No-vum Organum is an attempt towards fomewhat of the fame kind. But I much doubt, that if ever the mafons had it, they have now loſt it; fince fo few new arts have been lately invented, and fo many are wanted. The idea I have of fuch an art is, that it muſt be fomething proper to be applied in all the fciences generally, as algebra is in numbers, by the help of which, new rules of arithmetic are, and may be found.

(15) Preife.] It feems the mafons have great regard to the reputation as well as the profit of their order; fince they make it one reafon for not divulging an art in common, that it may do honour to the poffeffors of it. I think in this particular they

they fhew too much regard for their
own fociety, and too little for the reft of
mankind.

(16) Arte of keepyng fecrettes.] What
kind of an art this is, I can by no means
imagine.   But certainly fuch an art the
mafons muft have: For though, as fome
people fuppofe, they fhould have no fecret at all, even that muft be a fecret
which being difcovered would expofe
them to the higheft ridicule : and therefore it requires the utmoft caution to
conceal it.

(17) Arte of chaunges.] I know not
what this means, unlefs it be the tranf-
mutation of metals.

(18) Facultye of Abrac.] Here I am
utterly in the dark.

(19) Univerfelle longage of maconnes.]
An univerfal language has been much
defired by the learned of many ages.   It
is a thing rather to be wifhed than hoped
for. But it feems the mafons pretend to
have fuch a thing among them. If it be
                                       true,

true, I guefs it muft be fomething like the language of the Pantomimes among the ancient Romans, who are faid to be able, by figns only, to exprefs and deliver any oration intelligibly to men of all nations and languages. A man who has all thefe arts and advantages, is certainly in a condition to be envied: But we are told, that this is not the cafe with all mafons; for though thefe arts are among them, and all have a right and an opportunity to know them, yet fome want capacity, and others induftry to acquire them. However, of all their arts and fecrets, that which I moft defire to know is, " The fkylle of becommynge gude and parfyghte;" and I wifh it were communicated to all mankind, fince there is nothing more true than the beautiful fentence contained in the laft anfwer, " That the better men are, the more they love one another." Virtue having in itfelf fomething fo amiable as to charm the hearts of all that behold it.

A

A GLOSSARY,

To explain the old words in the foregoing Manuscript.

ALLEIN, only
 Alweys, always
Beithe, both
Commodytye, conveniency
Confrerie, fraternity
Faconnynge, forming
Fore-sayinge, prophecying
Freres, brethren
Headlye, chiefly
Hem plesethe, they please
Hemselfe, themselves
Her, there, their
Hereynne, therein
Herwyth, with it
Holpynge, beneficial
Kunne, know
Kunnynge, knowledge
Make gudde, are beneficial
Metynges, measures
Mote, may
Myddlelond, Mediterranean

      Myghte,

Myghte, power
Occasyonne, opportunity
Oder, or
Onelyche, only
Pernecessarye, absolutely necessary
Preise, honour
Recht, right
Reckenyngs, numbers
Sonderlyche, particularly
Skylle, knowledge
Wacksynge, growing
Werck, operation
Wey, way
Whereas, where
Woned, dwelt
Wunderwerckynge, working miracles
Wylde, savage
Wynnynge, gaining
Ynn, into

E R R A T A.

Of further interest

THE CRAFT
A History of English Freemasonry

John Hamill

Written for both Masonic and non-Masonic readers, *The Craft* traces the development of English Freemasonry from its obscure origins to the present day.

With clarity and authority John Hamill describes the various theories for the origins of Freemasonry, the development of the Grand Lodge system, the spread of Freemasonry abroad, the degrees and Orders additional to the Craft, and the development of Masonic charity.

For anyone with an interest in — or who is merely curious about — Freemasonry, *The Craft* provides straightforward, factual information about a subject that all too often has been prone to myth-making.

John Hamill was born in Wallsend-on-Tyne in 1947 and now lives in London. After reading History and Fine Art at Oxford Polytechnic and postgraduate Library Studies at Newcastle Polytechnic he joined the staff of the Grand Lodge Library and Museum in 1971, being appointed its Librarian and Curator in 1983. An internationally acknowledged authority on English Freemasonry, he was Master of the renowned Quatuor Coronati Lodge (of Research) No. 2706 during its centenary year.

A. E. WAITE: MAGICIAN OF MANY PARTS

R. A. Gilbert

Arthur Edward Waite (1857-1942) was unique: the only scholarly student of 'rejected knowledge' to emerge from the shadowy world of the Victorian occult revival. He introduced Eliphas Lévi to the English-speaking world, made the classics of alchemical literature available in English and, in 1903, resurrected the Hermetic Order of the Golden Dawn.

But Waite was no mere occultist. He was also a poet who corresponded with Robert Browning and W. B. Yeats; a Bohemian who created dramatic rituals for Arthur Machen; and a mystic who founded the Fellowship of the Rosy Cross — the esoteric order that so profoundly influenced Charles Williams. Besides these, and other, spheres of influence, all modern occult iconography is indebted to Waite for his Tarot pack, used by T. S. Eliot as the symbolic structure of *The Waste Land*.

In this, the first biography of Waite, R. A. Gilbert has drawn on an extensive range of published and unpublished sources, as well as on his own unrivalled knowledge of Waite's *milieu*, to present an engaging and accurate portrait of a truly remarkable man.

R. A. Gilbert read Philosophy and Psychology at the University of Bristol and is a well-known antiquarian bookdealer with an international reputation for his knowledge of Western esoteric ideas. His books include The Golden Dawn: Twilight of the Magicians *(1983),* The Golden Dawn Companion *(1986) and* The Treasure of Montségur *(with Walter Birks, 1987).*

THE GOLDEN DAWN COMPANION

A Guide to the History, Structure, and Workings of the Hermetic Order of the Golden Dawn

Compiled and introduced by R. A. Gilbert

The Hermetic Order of the Golden Dawn epitomized the paradox of an intellectual élite who rejected orthodox religion and yet remained within the social establishment of its day. The colourful story of these would-be magicians is well known to students of nineteenth-century social history, but the private archives on which the definitive history of the Order (Ellic Howe's *The Magicians of the Golden Dawn*) was based have remained inaccessible to scholars.

But now this material has been made available for study and the texts of both official and unofficial documents can at last be published. Here are the full texts of the Order's Constitution, Rules and Regulations, the Obligations of candidates for both the Outer and Inner Orders, the 'General Orders' of the R.R. et A.C., and the complete membership list from the official Address Book, together with detailed descriptions of the Temples, the Grade rituals, and the manuscripts that comprise the archives.

In addition, the original texts of the various theories of origin of the Golden Dawn are brought together for the first time, and there is a comprehensive bibliography of all printed material relating to the Order.

KING SOLOMON'S TEMPLE IN THE MASONIC TRADITION

Alex Horne

After studying an impressive array of biblical, historical and mythological traditions connected with the Temple and all the circumstances relating to its construction, Alex Horne wrote this absorbing work in the hope of arousing a deeper understanding and appreciation of Freemasonry, and to correct the inaccuracies and errors perpetrated in the many old quasi-historical narratives concerning the development of Masonry through the ages.

The result is a treatise in which persons, events, and localities take on a four-dimensional depth. We watch the fabric of the Temple being erected without the sound of axe, hammer, or any tool of iron. We follow the progress of stone from the quarries of Zeredathah, timber from the forest of Lebanon. And when the fourscore thousand 'hewers in the mountains and quarries' have completed their labours, we have an inkling why the various parts of the completed Temple fitted so exactly that the edifice appeared to have been created by the Supreme Architect of the Universe, rather than made by human hands.

Alex Horne, 33°, Ancient and Accepted Scottish Rite, S.J., USA, is a leading Masonic scholar and a Member of Quatuor Coronati Lodge No. 2076, the Premier Lodge of Masonic Research.

MASONIC CLASSICS SERIES
Series Editor: John Hamill,
Librarian of the United Grand Lodge of England

THE ROYAL MASONIC CYCLOPAEDIA

Edited by Kenneth R. H. Mackenzie
Introduced by R. A. Gilbert and John Hamill

The Royal Masonic Cyclopaedia was first issued in six parts at intervals between 1875 and 1877, a much-needed encyclopaedic handbook designed specifically for English Freemasons.

But it was more than that. In the guise of a masonic reference book, Mackenzie and his fellow contributors (Benjamin Cox, F. G. Irwin, W. R. Woodman, John Yarker, and other members of the *Societas Rosicruciana in Anglia*) distilled the essence of Victorian esoteric thought, and in so doing unwittingly provided a primary sourcebook for the history of the nineteenth-century Occult Revival.

This is the first modern reprint of this celebrated work, which concentrated on the border between the more exotic high degrees of Freemasonry and occultism proper and reflected Mackenzie's lifelong enthusiasm for hermetic philosophy in all its branches.

The *Cyclopaedia*'s greatest influence, however, was on those esoterically inclined Freemasons who created the Hermetic Order of the Golden Dawn, making it an essential text for anyone who wishes to understand the relationship between Freemasonry and occultism in the Victorian age.

MASONIC FACTS AND FICTIONS

Comprising A New Theory of the Origin of the 'Antient' Grand Lodge

Henry Sadler
Introduced by John Hamill

As a Masonic historian, Henry Sadler was meticulous in his attention to detail and scrupulous in his attention to fact. The quality of his research earned him the accolade, in 1903, of full membership of Quatuor Coronati Lodge No. 2706, the most prestigious Lodge of Masonic research, and this in turn led him to the blue ribband of Masonic scholarships, the Mastership of that Lodge.

Masonic Facts and Fictions (1887) is a seminal work in the historiography of English Freemasonry. Although Sadler subtitled his work 'A New Theory of the Origin of the "Antient" Grand Lodge', so persuasive is his critical examination of the evidence that few today would question his conclusion that the Antient Grand Lodge did not develop from a schism in the Premier Grand Lodge but had its origins in a group of unattached Masons of Irish origin.

Sadler was breaking new ground not just with his theory, but by discussing the Antients at all. Snobbishly dismissed by Premier Grand Lodge as tradesmen and menials of little interest, the Antients continued to be ignored down to our own time by all but Sadler whose book contains a wealth of information from Grand Lodge and private Lodge archives that is not readily available elsewhere.

THE BOOK OF THE LODGE

George Oliver
Introduced by Richard Sandbach

The third (1864) edition of *The Book of the Lodge* considerably enlarged the two previous editions, published in 1849 and 1856. The author, the Revd George Oliver D.D., was an Anglican priest known to his fellow-masons as the 'sage of Masonry' and was an acknowledged authority on Masonic history, symbolism, and ritual.

The Book of the Lodge deals first with building and furnishing a Lodge room and there are further chapters on the working of a Lodge, the duties of its officers, and the symbolism of the 'Tracing Boards' and 'Working Tools' of the three degrees.

The practices described are often those of the eighteenth century; but throughout shines Oliver's conviction that, even after the attempted removal of all Christian references from the ritual by the Duke of Sussex, Freemasonry remained in every way compatible with Christianity.

Richard Sandbach is a retired solicitor living in Peterborough. He read Law at St John's College, Cambridge and entered Freemasonry in 1949. He is currently Provincial Grand Master, Northamptonshire and Huntingdonshire, Member of Quatuor Coronati Lodge No. 2076, and Honorary Member of the Lodge of Research, No. 2479, Leicester.

ILLUSTRATIONS OF MASONRY

William Preston
Introduced by Colin Dyer

William Preston (1742-1818), although a controversial figure, was the foremost Masonic teacher of his day. His *Illustrations of Masonry* resulted from a gala performance of his catechetical lectures in which the nature, ceremonies, and symbolism of Freemasonry were explained.

Working for a number of years as an assistant to the Grand Secretary, Preston was at the centre of the Masonic world in England and had access to the records of the Craft which enabled him to add an historical section to his *Illustrations.* Pirate editions appeared in the USA and were used by T. S. Webb as the basis for his *Monitor,* which became the standard Masonic handbook in the USA in the early part of the nineteenth century.

For anyone interested in the history and development of English Craft ritual Preston's *Illustrations* is essential reading. For those interested in the history of English Freemasonry it provides a valuable commentary on eighteenth-century Freemasonry.

Colin Dyer is a Past Master of the prestigious Quatuor Coronati Lodge and was Prestonian Lecturer in 1973. An internationally recognized authority on the history of the English Craft ritual, he was for many years a Committee member and Secretary of the Emulation Lodge of Improvement, guardian of the most widely used working of the Ritual. He has been a Common Councilman and Chief Commoner in the City of London.